A Special Education in Anxiety

Bradley Smith

Printed in the United States by Create Space.

Book and cover design by Eric Bodiroga.

Dedication

To my wife, and truly better half, Jenn.
To my mom, Lois Smith, who helped with
too many aspects of this book to list.
Finally, to my students, past and present,
who have made teaching the only
profession I could ever imagine doing.

CHAPTER ONE

I NOD MY HEAD and smile widely as I extend an open hand in front of Justin, hoping for a high five in return.

Justin, breaks his upward gaze and looks my direction. Soon though, his eyes shift back to the old fluorescent lights directly above his seat. Justin continues staring, blinking at regular intervals, his mind clearly someplace else. Sometimes when I sit next to him I hear bits of dialogue from a movie, "scripting," or the humming of a familiar theme song, but right now he is looking off in silence.

I keep my hand extended, and after a few seconds Justin takes the prompt and lifts his hand slowly, as if an invisible weight was attached to his wrist, and drops his palm onto mine. "That was an awesome job, Justin! Great job, man!"

Suddenly, without any warning, Justin's expression changes. His dark pupils—a strong contrast to his bright blue eyes—have grown almost twice in size, and his forehead crinkles simultaneously. He begins a low, groaning sound. His moan quickly changes to a high-pitched shriek, as if electricity has just shot through the synapses in his brain. This scream is not new to this classroom, but it still makes my shoulders jerk involuntarily every time.

Justin looks over at me. His moods can often be hard to read, but the one expression that is obvious is when he is feeling intense pain. Once the excruciating headache has started, experience has taught us that there is not much you can do for him in the moment; you and he just have to ride it out together.

What started with Justin banging his right palm rhythmically on the table has now switched to a more gruesome sight: he takes the palm of his right hand, raises it to about six inches from his face, pauses, and then starts to strike the bridge of his nose. He has already landed a few blows and is looking to increase the power behind each strike. Using his left hand almost as reinforcement for his right wrist, Justin makes one last scream, and then begins to slam his supported right hand, like a jackhammer, blow after blow to where the cartilage meets bone.

"Jan, throw me Justin's cushion!" I shout out.

Jan, already halfway to the foam pad before I give the direction, swoops it up and tosses it to me. I catch it, get down on one knee, and with one swinging motion I get it safely tucked between Justin's palm and his already swelling nose. With my right hand holding the cushion now securely in place and my left arm up trying to protect myself from harm, Justin gives the cushion a few good whacks, testing its strength. It does its job well, but he does not like that we have deterred him from the function these punches are somehow providing.

I am still kneeling next to Justin. As I turn to ask Barbara, our other Instructional Assistant, to take the rest of the kids outside, I shift my focus away from Justin and lower my left arm. I should have known better. When I look back, his eyes are locked on me. Before I can pull my arm back up to protect myself, he is already following through, striking his palm into my left temple. The impact stuns me, and fuzzy lines impair my vision for a split second. I regain control and get myself into a safer position.

Getting behind Justin's chair, I yell, "Barbara, get the kids out quicker!" They need to clear the room for safety, and they have no reason to see one of their classmates, and friends, in this emotional state.

I remember to add a little more tact to my second request: "Barb, if you could turn the lights out, too, that would be great." These cheap fluorescent classroom lights are not good for anyone with stabbing pain behind his eyes, as anyone who suffers from migraines knows, so switching them off for Justin at this moment is a must.

I rise to my feet and move behind Justin with my right hip perpendicular to his shoulder blades. This is the protective stance I should have started with from the beginning. As I stand out of harm's reach, I realize he has no protection now, the original pad having dropped next to his chair. I look at Jan, and don't have to say anything—she is already moving toward the cushion to get ready to shield Justin from any further injury. Justin glances down and recognizes that the cushion is on the floor, giving him the unrestricted shot he was looking for.

Before Jan and I can do anything, Justin winds back, turns his palm inward, his left hand grasping the right for extra strength, and lands a direct blow to the bridge of his nose. The thunderous pop at impact is the horrifying climax to the whole episode. The bright red blood oozing from his nose stands out shockingly against his pale skin and begins to drip rapidly onto his Harry Potter T-shirt and blue jeans. You can see the precipitating pain and frustration release from his body, gone as quickly as it came. He has moved into his recovery phase. I'm not sure if it was the impact of the blow, the initial pain ceasing, or some aspect of self-injury I just don't understand, but something that was wrong in Justin's body has now been made right, though in a frightening, dangerous way.

How I wish he was able to tell us what bothered him so much, and why pain had to be part of his solution. I ask Jan to stay with him for a second as I grab some gloves and gauze. We go through our established "Justin protocol," which involves a phone call to the family, a nurse's visit, and an incident report completion.

"Hey, it's okay, buddy—we will try to figure this out, I promise," I say softly in the darkened room. Justin is plugging his ears with his two pointer fingers and is back to making the original moaning sound, bowing his head and rocking back and forth. Though he seems calm, one of my gloved hands is holding gauze to his nose, while the other hand still instinctively tightens around the cushion in case it is needed a second time. I can hear his breathing slowing, and he is saying, "*Owww,*" in a pained whisper.

While we wait for the nurse, Jan walks over and rubs Justin's back. "Poor guy," she says sympathetically. After a moment of silence, out of the blue Jan turns to me and says, "You know my mom always said I'd have made a good office receptionist. She said I was good with people, and organized, too. I can picture myself being kind of like Pam in *The Office.*"

For the first time since the start of this most recent emergency, I smile. "C'mon, Jan, you know you'd be bored in any job compared to this one. I always say you are the glue that holds this classroom together."

Jan's expression reminds me of Justin's earlier one as she looks off toward the ceiling. I think she is legitimately giving weight to my comment. "That's nice of you to say. Some stuff I suppose people are just meant to do."

The nurse appears in the doorway and comes in to check on Justin's current condition as we wait for his mom. She looks a little nervous—unsure if Justin might lash out at her. I try to reassure her that the worst should be over. As I talk with her, I can feel my heart rate starting to increase, my body temperature heating up, and my breathing starting to become more shallow. *Oh no,* I think, *here it comes.*

*   *   *   *

Sitting in my Toyota Corolla parked in front of the church, I watch the rain splat on the windshield. It's been non-stop today. I've got five minutes to kill before my appointment. For some reason my eyes are drawn to one specific drop, slowly crawling down the window and then colliding with a stagnant bead. They fuse together and slide down the window and out of sight. The drops bring to mind, actually, the reason I'm here at a church on a Thursday after work to begin with, although the location feels uncomfortable, since I haven't attended a church in over four years.

The water-speckled window reminds me of the beads of sweat that form whenever I am put in a situation that makes me feel socially anxious. For those who haven't experienced this feeling, the resulting perspiration is not like what would naturally occur on a scorching hot day, or what you would earn playing one-on-one for an hour at the gym. These are evil droplets that sprout on my forehead like a virus whenever I feel trapped in a conversation with someone. It's not the person. It's not the conversation. It's an out-of-nowhere reaction that gives me a hyper-vigilant yet fuzzyheaded, dream-like feeling. I have been having this response four to six times a day, and that is the reason for my every other week visits here. While my forehead fills with sweat, my self-confidence and self-esteem are getting sucked dry.

*   *   *   *

Until four years ago, raindrops on a car window would have reminded me of the rainy days we would frequently experience in my hometown of Portland, Oregon, on the west coast. That was before my first social anxiety panic attack. I try to tell myself, *It's a bigger deal in your head than it is to other people.* But these messages never seem to change the outcome, and I still feel the same level of defeat and despair following each attack. The clammy shirt sticking to my body is the physical reminder that reinforces the belief that I won't be getting better any time soon. I know if I just didn't care what people were thinking about me that half the problem would be solved—but for some reason I always care.

*   *   *   *

I would like to think of myself as a giving person, someone who puts family, friends, and my students first. However, I'm starting to think the worst part about an anxiety disorder is that it warps your normal perspective so you can't stop thinking about yourself. You have a social encounter with a co-worker, then, after sweating through the interaction, you replay the same conversation in your head twenty times or more afterwards. It's as if your mind's mental real estate— which used to drift toward good memories of the past, upcoming weekend plans, or a catchy new song getting lots of radio play, now goes to the same set of questions:

How did my conversation go?
Did I make her feel uncomfortable with our talk?
Did he notice I was starting to get sweaty?
How was my eye contact?
Was it too much?
Was it too little?
How was my comment?
Did it seem like a comment I used to make?
Am I getting better, or worse?

My fears and worries infiltrate my dreams, too, as conversations and social situations get replayed at night, but with bizarre twists. Sound sleep eludes me. I'm exhausted.

I once heard a podcast about people who struggle with blushing. One story was about a college freshman who got so engulfed by his fear of blushing that the more he thought about it the more he tried to avoid situations he couldn't escape once he started to blush. He would take the stairs instead of the elevator, or go to places with darker lighting. Finally, one day he wrote a five-page letter to his parents saying he loved them but was just too weary from trying to figure out how he was going to make it through the day with this constant fear. He then threw himself out of his apartment building. When I heard the conclusion of the story, I shuddered. I don't entertain thoughts about ending my life, but his struggle and pain hit way too close to home.

*   *   *   *

I pull my focus away from the raindrops, forcing myself to stop the mental loops of "what ifs" regarding my upcoming social encounter. I look past the beads of water, and, like one of those Magic Eye pictures that comes into focus, I can see the simple brick church with a white steeple. The church sign board has 'HOPE BAPTIST' written at the top with a cross, a Bible, and the message:

JANUARY 15, 2012
EVERYONE NEEDS
SOME GRACE

It begins to pour. I swing open the car door and sprint toward the church, making cuts and avoiding giant puddles like one of Tom Brady's shifty wide receivers escaping would-be tacklers. I burst into the foyer with less than half of my shirt soaked through. I grimly think, *At least it's from the rain and not a boatload of sweating.*

CHAPTER TWO

IT WAS ABOUT FOUR years ago that I decided I no longer seemed to fit inside the walls of a church. As I near the pastor's office door, I think of the reason why I've come back to a place I tried my best to avoid for so many years. After opening up and talking about my "anxiety problem" to an old childhood friend, Dallas, he said he knew a friend who got a lot of good support from this pastor. He said Pastor Tim was really engaged during the sessions and genuinely seemed to care about helping him. I was a little hesitant to call Tim that first time, especially since I didn't go to his church. I honestly figured he would just say that his counseling was for church members only. I wouldn't blame him. There's only so much time we all have to give, but Tim said no such thing, and he immediately set up a meeting for later that same week.

Whenever I meet with Tim for one of our sessions, he greets me with a disarming smile and looks me right in the eyes. This would normally jumpstart my anxiety cycle, but the guy knows my story, and finds a way to keep my social fears at bay. Pastor Tim has to be in his early 50s, tall and wiry, like someone who played competitive sports in his younger days. He has the clean-cut look down—his graying hair neatly parted to the left, a navy sweater vest over a white buttoned-down shirt, and charcoal slacks. Fortunately, his personality doesn't coincide with his somewhat stuffy attire.

This week he starts the conversation by talking about the Celtics Big Three and whether they have one more championship run in them. Tim is very into the fact that Paul Pierce is only a couple of games away from passing Larry Bird as second on the all-time Celtics scoring list. "That guy, man, he is The Truth!" I laugh at Tim's passion and love for his hometown team.

Every session with Tim starts in a similar manner. He gets me in a talkative mood by going to the subjects that are most comfortable for me. Then, skillfully, like a Rajon Rondo bounce pass, he smoothly transitions to more serious topics. He gets me sharing about my week, then asks, "I remember two weeks ago you were saying it had been particularly bad when a student's parent visited the classroom and you felt trapped, like you couldn't escape the situation. How have things been going at work?" Tim is very good at remembering details of past conversations and bringing the right ones up to explore further. It makes me feel like I was really heard during our time together. I appreciate that.

"Yeah, this week has been more of the same," I respond. "This time it was one of my students' grandmothers who came by the classroom to pick him up. As soon as she entered the room, it was like my forehead was getting primed to start sweating. I could feel it all over—warm prickles hitting my body, but especially my forehead. I said 'hello' to her really fast and pretended I needed to do something else in the classroom. I tried to escape so I wouldn't get stuck in a long conversation with sweat pouring down my face."

"What happened? Did you get away?"

"Well, no, she was pretty quick for an old woman," I chuckle. "She stayed on my tail and asked me question after question that required a response." I picture the scene in my mind, facing Devonte's grandma, and dripping like a Popsicle in an oven.

"So did things get better?" Tim asks, looking for a trace of something positive in the story.

"No, I pretty much poured sweat the whole time. I don't know what she was thinking. If I were in her shoes, I'd wonder, 'What's wrong with this guy? It's not that hot in here.' The conversation did eventually end, though, and when she and Devonte finally left the room, I was so relieved. But you know what's weird? As soon as they left, part of me wished that they would come right back. It drives me crazy when someone leaves and I'm not able to end the conversation on a good, or at least normal, note. I need some way for that person to know that things are okay, otherwise I'm just going to dwell on that conversation nonstop for days."

Tim and I hash that out a while longer, and then my mind drifts to a dream I had the other night. "You know what I wanted to run by you, Tim . . . this dream that I had earlier in the week that is still weighing on me."

Tim smiles and says, "Okay, but just so you know I'm not claiming to be an interpreter of dreams." He holds out his hand and beckons, "But please, share." I have a feeling that stuff like dreams is more interesting to him than he lets on, though. His body bends slightly closer to me, and his eyes brighten. I appreciate how Tim is always okay with the way I jump around in conversations. I know I am not the most linear thinker or talker, so just the fact that he lets me take the conversation in different directions puts me at ease.

I pause for a second to formulate my thoughts, then say, "So, it was one of those strangely normal dreams, the kind where you wake up and it takes a second to figure out if you were having a dream or just replaying a past memory. But, yeah, after this dream I felt real despair, as bad as I've ever had."

Tim nods, signaling me to go on. I don't usually like to dominate the conversation, even in counseling, but the story comes spilling out of me: "So I was having some sort of special dinner at my parents' old house. My mom and dad and my brother and his wife were there, so the timeline of my dream didn't make a lot of sense, now that I think about it. We sold and moved out of that house when I was in second grade, and I haven't dreamt about it in a long time.

"Anyways, along with my family, my high school and college friends were there as well—some guys from the high school basketball team, some friends from the dorms, a lot of guys and girls I haven't talked to in real life for quite a while. Then there was this girl that was sitting two seats away from me who I couldn't quite see because the guy next to me kept blocking my view. It was one of those weird feelings, though, that you only have in dreams, that you just know even without seeing her that she is sweet and beautiful. I could hear her laugh, but no matter how I twisted my body, that guy right beside me made it impossible for me to see her. It kind of reminded me of that scene with Jim Carrey in *Eternal Sunshine of the Spotless Mind* where, no matter what he tried, he wasn't able to see the face of Elijah Wood's character, whose back was turned away from him. Have you seen that movie, Tim?"

The pastor shakes his head, so I don't expand on the comparison.

"Anyways," I continue, "friends from all the different eras of my life kept coming by my chair, and we talked about old times, and shared stories and inside jokes that I had long-ago forgotten. Every conversation seemed to end with a good laugh or a slap on the back, and the dinner continued. In my dream I remember my stomach literally hurting from all the full-body laughter. We kept eating—it seemed like a huge Thanksgiving feast or something, then for some reason, I stood up and asked if I could make a toast. I looked all around the table at each person—eye to eye. I felt confident and happy that all these people I knew and loved were there. The only person I couldn't make eye contact with was the girl who was engaged in conversation with one of my old high school friends seated on the other side of her. Although her back was to me, I could hear her laughing and see her shoulders shaking.

"Somehow in my dream I realized that seeing her face was a lost cause at this point, so I turned my attention back to the toast. I raised my glass and said, 'To my favorite people in the world. To all the good times we had, and all the good times I know we will have in the future. Cheers!' Everyone raised their glasses and shouted, 'Cheers!' and they were all smiling, laughing and clinking glasses.

"Then, all of a sudden, without any transition, I woke up. My chest didn't have that warm feeling that I felt during my speech, though. It felt tight, and I literally gasped for air."

Tim settles back, trying to piece together and process what I've shared. He clasps his hands in front of him, lowers his eyes in thought, then looks up at me and says, "I don't understand, Michael. What about the dream had such a paralyzing effect on you? A dream spending time with family and friends is fairly common. So is being at your childhood home and eating foods you love. What about this dream disturbed you so much when you woke up? Was it the girl?"

"No, it wasn't her, although I have to admit I was very sorry I never got to see her face. I guess the problem was that the dream was so amazing."

Tim pauses, giving space for me to explain further.

"The dream reminded me of everything that it seems like I'll never get to do again," I continue, "joking with friends, laughing uncontrollably . . ."

"Being in the moment," Tim offers.

"Yeah, none of that seems possible with people now," I say while looking down. "I barely even remember what those things feel like. A night with a couple drinks is as close as I can get to 'feeling like normal,' but it's like I'm an imposter. It's not the real me. It's not how I used to be. Not like in my dream."

"Sorry, Michael, I probably could have put that together more. Guess I failed as your dream interpreter. Sorry I'm no Joseph," Tim remarks with a stab at church humor. "I see where you are coming from, though. Reminds me in a way of a war veteran who has lost his legs, but in his dream he's running around a baseball diamond like his pre-military days. The dream itself is beautiful, but the pain of reaching for his legs when he wakes up tears him apart. People say you don't know joy without suffering, but maybe the reverse is also true—you don't know suffering without first knowing joy. I don't know . . .

"Michael, is there only one goal for you at this point? Can you only have a fulfilled and happy life if you can reach that point again of being anxiety-free? Or at least however you defined it in the past? What if you don't, though? What if that is no longer an option?"

"That's what I'm afraid of!" I snap. I am surprised by my harsh tone because I'm usually careful not to offend people.

Tim doesn't seem ruffled by my abrupt response. "The question I'm going to leave with you, Michael, and what I want you to think about is this: Is it possible that there are multiple layers of good for you? Let's say you have that dream again, but, for the sake of argument, this time you start sweating in the middle of your toast, or that girl has an engagement ring on her finger, or conversations with old friends don't come as easily as you hoped they would. Does that mean that the whole experience that felt so unbelievably good in your first dream is now a totally negative one? Same people, same experiences, just things not quite so perfect? Would it be a nightmare that you would be relieved to wake up from or a dream that still had some good parts?

"You don't have to have an answer, but think about it for next time. I want you to challenge yourself this week to see how you label each experience. If you had a line of drawers"—Tim pretends to lay five drawers side by side—"which categories could the experiences go into? Is there only one drawer for good experiences, and another one for bad?" He points to the left and the right. "Or are there several drawers in between, not labeled, that you have been neglecting these last couple of years? I'm curious."

As I get up to leave, Pastor Tim says he will be praying for me. Thinking about my sharp response earlier, I apologize if I sounded rude. Tim gives me a reassuring smile and says he didn't even notice. I'm glad I spoke up, though, and confirmed that he wasn't offended—otherwise I know I would dwell on it for days.

CHAPTER THREE

I WILL ALWAYS HAVE a soft spot for my seventh-grade student Molly, whose autism impacts her pretty severely. This is our second year together. Various sights, sounds, and touch distress her, but, unlike Justin, who shares similar sensory processing issues, Molly's reactions are not injurious to herself or others. When a stimulus overwhelms her, she gets a look of terror that reminds me of a panicky child who can't find her mom at the grocery store. The fear flashes on her face, and, like Justin, she will express her feelings in wordless groans. She will rock back and forth, trying to regain control of her body and her emotions, and after some time this repetitive motion seems to bring her back to a regulated state.

Molly usually speaks in short, one-word utterances: "Yes." "No." "Go." "Bye." However, don't let her lack of verbal utterances fool you into thinking she is not paying attention. Molly is very aware of her surroundings. Her eyes are always documenting everything in the environment around her. If a trashcan in the back of the classroom gets moved six inches away from its original spot before the students arrive, she will notice it within three seconds of entering the room and frantically powerwalk over to put it in its proper place, rocking her body as she takes each step. Her world, if even only temporarily, is restored to normal for the time being.

After situations like that, I'm reminded of a beach ball that gets punctured by a pin and slowly deflates back to its natural flat shape. It is like that with Molly's body. As she releases the tension and anxiety, you can almost see the adrenaline leaving her body. I feel for Molly's struggle—and Justin's, too—because I can relate to that feeling of anxiety flooding your system. I know my anxieties are no comparison to the obstacles they face in almost every setting, and Molly has far less language to navigate this unpredictable world, but she has found her ways of coping. She brings DVD cases and special toys from home, which she lines up on her desk in a very particular order. For some reason, like the trashcan, having those items from home in a specific place provides a certain level of comfort for Molly.

Part of me as a teacher thinks I need to be firm and tell Molly she can't bring these objects to school, and hopefully lessen the hold these items have on her. I think of scenarios where a DVD case gets lost and we are pretty much all screwed then, or a fire drill happens and she is unable to leave quickly because she is worried about her toys. Her need to have the figurines and cases out there is something I originally wanted to wean her off of, however, for now I see that she needs them as supports. They bring order, predictability, and comfort so she can focus on other things. My personal supports have been positive mantras, breaks to regain my composure, and my meds. So, if I took those items away from her, it would be the equivalent of saying the way I deal with anxiety is appropriate but her ordered DVDs and toys are not acceptable. Once I think of it in that light, I stop trying to figure out a way to change her.

*   *   *   *

So how did my story start? What precipitated the shift onto the distressing path I now find myself on?

It all began on a flight home for Christmas Break. It had been a particularly rough winter that senior year in Boston, and I was looking forward to heading back west. Shortly after takeoff from Logan Airport, the stewardess came up to me and offered me a package of those delicious Biscoff Biscuits and a drink. She was very friendly, and even offered me an extra pack of Biscoffs—I think she could tell that I was a college kid, too poor to pay for an actual airplane box meal. While I thanked her for the free food, a thought formed that I have talked about in counseling and reflected on for the past four years. The thought started innocently enough—*That is a nice person for offering me food.* As she reached over the man asleep in the aisle seat, my thoughts consciously went to eye contact for the first time in my life: *She has really strong eye contact. I've never noticed that about people before. Is that normal?* My "thank you" was the end of our actual conversation, but the conversation in my head was just beginning. *Is what I was giving her for eye contact normal? Am I sending any type of flirtatious vibe, or anything like that? The last thing I want to do is make her feel uncomfortable.*

That last thought—"I don't want to make her feel uncomfortable"—clicked in my brain and got slammed shut like the door of Andy Dufresne's cell at the beginning of *The Shawshank Redemption.* I didn't know it at the time, but my life and my ability to relate or talk with people would be completely altered from that point, December 15, 2008, forward.

I remember stepping off the plane and saying "Hi" to my parents. I worried about eye contact with my mom for the first time in my life. My mom, of all people! Did I really have to worry about my mom thinking I was overusing eye contact, or acting creepy all of a sudden? The thoughts kept on firing, though. *Was what I was doing normal? Could my mom and dad tell that I was acting differently?* I started to sweat from these thoughts for the first time. My parents noticed the beads of perspiration forming and asked if I was okay. I blamed it on starting to feel a little sick on the plane.

During the Winter Break I saw the movie *Inception*, which was a bad call on my part, considering what was starting to form in my own mind. The protagonist, Dom Cobb, played by Leonardo DiCaprio, said, "What is the most resilient parasite? Bacteria? A virus? No, it's an idea. Resilient and highly contagious. Once an idea has taken hold of the brain, it's almost impossible to eradicate."

Day by day it felt as if there was another person in my life that I couldn't talk to because my mind would check them off as someone with whom I had had an awkward social eye contact moment. Once you were on that list, you either stayed there, or I had to know that everything was okay between us. I tried to reassure myself, *They don't think I'm creepy or weird.* Every day, though, it felt like I had ruined another relationship. Soon I began to avoid meeting up with people in person, resorting to phone calls and texts. This felt like the only option available if I still wanted to have friends in any form.

I kept wondering, *What don't I understand about nonverbal communication? Is my eye contact so long that they are noticing? Is it too short where they think I am ashamed or hiding something?* I started to keep my eyes closed a fraction longer with each blink. I think

I was hoping to have less time to view the expressions of the people around me.

My dad was the first to notice these prolonged blinks. "Why are you closing your eyes like that?" he asked once at dinner, sounding confused. I wasn't ready to talk to anyone about this one yet, so I just said my eyes were feeling funny and I kept my head down, focusing on my plate of half-eaten mashed potatoes.

Coming back to school in January, I was cautiously optimistic that this was just some kind of aberrant episode in my life and that everything would return to normal. That idea actually gave me some hope. However, it didn't take long to realize this wouldn't be a short-lived problem.

While attending my final classes to become a Special Education teacher, I was trying my best to get through student teaching without having to confess these irrational notions to anyone. Many would not realize that I was slowly pulling myself away from daily life with friends, often blaming it on lesson plans that needed to get done or reflection papers that were part of my coursework. It was the perfect out, and I was constantly using those excuses. The thoughts hadn't gone away with my school routine back in place, and I started to feel physically sick thinking about the new anxiety-filled situations around the corner each day. I did call in sick a lot during those last ten weeks of student teaching—a cardinal sin for a teacher in training. I blamed it on the brutal east-coast weather causing the flu, but I knew my stomach pains and light-headedness could be traced back to that thought that had been planted in my brain on that plane ride home.

After sweating it through senior year and more student teaching, I started to pick up bad habits. I stopped wearing contact lenses so that I couldn't see as well and wouldn't be able to view people's eyes while talking to them. That plan was not sustainable, though, as I realized it was very hard to be a good teacher when I was often unable to differentiate students, and everyone in the hallway looked like variations of the same fuzzy blob.

Around this time I started to think some truly bizarre thoughts, such as: *What if I had my eyes removed? It would cause me to be blind, but at least I could be able to be around people again, and actually be present instead of looking for the moment where I could retreat to the bathroom to splash cold water on my face.* I didn't honestly entertain the eye-removal idea—I knew it was crazy—but being in a constant state of fear started to make ideas like that seem a little less crazy. It frightened me that I was even going that direction with my thoughts.

CHAPTER FOUR

IT'S MONDAY, AND THE first student through the door is Stevie. He comes bolting past the A113 sign next to the door and gives me a greeting that has become one of the consistent highlights of my day. "Hiii, Miiisster Sniiiiff!" he says, stretching out the vowels like taffy.

"Hey, what's up, Stevie?" I respond. "How's it going? How was your weekend?"

Stevie responds back with another super-positive greeting but not quite an answer to any of the questions. "Hiii Miister Sniiiff!" I give Stevie a low-five and give the weekend question another shot.

"Hiiii Miiister Sniiiff!" he says one last time, with an even bigger smile.

"All right, Stevie, thanks for the always awesome greeting. But the big question was, 'How was your weekend?' "

He shrugs, and I see that he is having a hard time recalling the weekend, so I give him a few ideas. "You usually have pretty good weekends. Did you go to the inside pool or the library this weekend?"

"Yeaa," Stevie responds back.

I press forward, asking him, "Which one? The pool?"

"Yes!" he says with more enthusiasm.

Judging from his tone, I think I'm on the right track. "Did you go down the twisting water slide, Stevie? Your mom told me at Back-to-School Night how much you love going on that."

"Yes!" he exclaims with excitement, connecting the dots of his weekend. I used to try to correct Stevie's pronunciation of my name each morning. The variation has grown on me now, though, and I would be genuinely disappointed if he were to stop calling me Mr. Sniff.

Stevie is one of two students in our classroom who has Down syndrome, along with his friend Stephanie. He is fairly short in stature, with brown freckles that are highly concentrated around his cheeks and work their way back to his almond-shaped eyes. His freckles match the color of his short, light brown hair.

Stevie likes to keep things casual and often wears sweatpants and athletic shoes with Velcro in place of laces. He is the official greeter of everyone who enters Room A113. Though he gets a mixed bag of responses to his morning greetings from the other students in the classroom, one of his best traits is his persistence. He will keep at it until he receives a greeting back from each classmate that is satisfactory to him. He doesn't think his friend is not responding because he has a cognitive delay or is tired or doesn't want to say "hi." He always assumes the best in others. Stevie keeps at it until everyone says "hello" to him in the best way he or she knows or is able.

If the kids in our class were a sports team, Stevie would be the high-energy, good-chemistry guy—a player who brings out the best in all of his teammates—the 2008 Celtics' Kevin Garnett of our Special Education classroom, I suppose.

Justin, a student completely content to be by himself, thinking his own thoughts, has been worn down by Stevie's daily greeting routine. After two months, Justin will raise his hand on cue for a high-five as he sees Stevie approaching him in the morning. I'm so proud of my kids whenever I see that moment like that—no adult intervention, just two students doing a typical middle-school thing in their own way.

Molly, on the other hand, hasn't quite fully embraced Stevie as part of her morning routine. Part of it is due to her autism and her aversion to touch, and, as Stevie approaches, I see her rocking back and forth, showing signs that her anxiety is starting to rise. After a first unsuccessful greeting, Stevie tries it again one more time: "Hiii Molllyyyy!" Now she gives him a quick "hi," which is good enough for Stevie today. Molly transitions away and starts to straighten the classroom items that have been unintentionally changed by the custodian overnight.

Stevie comes up to Stephanie and says, "Hi Stephanieee!" You can find Stephanie wearing one of her dozen One Direction shirts most days of the week. In addition to her boy-band gear, she usually wears a pair of comfortable looking jeans, and her auburn brown hair is pulled back in a ponytail. One time she brought in a picture from her fifth-grade graduation last year, in which she was wearing a beautiful white prom-style dress. You could tell she was really proud of her appearance, and I think it's great that she feels good about herself, whether she is going with relaxed jeans and a T-shirt or dressed up for a special occasion.

"Hi Ste-vie," Stephanie says, breaking up the syllables in his name with her slightly deeper voice. They start to give each other a hug, but, sweet as it is, I have to remind them that we just give high-fives and fist-pounds to our friends at school. They go in for one more hug, and I have to prompt them again with a little sterner voice. I hate to be the enforcer during these feel-good moments, but I've learned I have to draw clear lines so the kids will be safe in other settings.

I had a student during my first year of teaching who would hug his friends, and it was great, but one day on a community outing he got overly excited and hugged a random 40-year-old man riding the T. Maybe the man reminded him of his dad, but the guy was clearly not the friendly, good-hearted type. He swore first at the boy and then at me, then barked, "Get this retard off of me!" I've learned some Bostonians can be pretty brusque, but there's no excuse for someone being this big of a jerk.

Stevie and Stephanie adjust their greeting to a high-five and then walk off together to start their morning work. The two are, as Tom Hanks said in *Forrest Gump,* "like peas and carrots." They've been in the same class for five years now, and their families are close friends, too. Whenever one of them is absent, the other is obviously dismayed. The biggest tears I ever saw came when Stevie realized Stephanie was going to be gone for the third day in a row. Even though they actually have only a few verbal exchanges each day, there is a definite security for both of them in being in the same space every day.

*   *   *   *

This classroom is a special place where someone can walk in and instantly pick up on a different kind of atmosphere. I don't mean surface level differences like an abundance of visual schedules, color-coded notebooks, communication systems, and work samples that may seem primary for a middle school. I'm not even talking about students with slightly atypical physical features or the humming that can often become the soundtrack of our classroom. There is another variance that you just don't find in any other classroom at Twin Oaks. I've thought about it, and have come to the conclusion that both the students of A113 and the peer tutors all follow an unspoken agreement that this is a judgment-free zone. I believe there are very few places, if any, where you do not feel judged while in middle school. For some, this might be the only time over the course of their school day where they get to breathe the refreshing air of full-acceptance.

Self-worth here isn't measured by how attractive you are, the awesomeness of your weekend plans, or if you own the latest iPhone. I love it when our eighth-grade Language Arts teacher, Ms. Liu, sends some of her students to our class to help our students. I get to observe firsthand how those protective middle school walls start to come down day by day. It just sort of happens. Those kids come in and connect, and bring something out of our students that I can't as an adult, and our students connect and bring something out of the peers tutors that no other individual in this school could ever do. Something symbiotic happens, and nine times out of ten everyone walks away better from the whole experience. I know that was my story ten years ago, when I was a peer tutor back at Southlake High School, volunteering in that role for the first time.

* * * *

Last school year, I found out from our counselor that one of our peer tutors, Cory, was using drugs, and her home life was a wreck. She seemed to wear a lot of black, which matched her long dyed hair and thick eyeliner. Hidden behind her tough exterior, though, was a tenderness toward kids who were marginalized. I saw her smile appear only when she worked with Justin.

I don't know what it was, but the two of them hit it off. Within weeks Justin worked harder for her than he had done for me in two years. When he would rock and moan, she wouldn't flinch or shrink back, but just stay there quietly, sometimes slowly and rhythmically patting his hand. Justin one time returned the gesture and moved Cory's hand from his hand to his ear, I think communicating to her that his head hurt. If I knew then what I do now, I would have gotten some distance between her and Justin for her safety, but this was before his first hitting incident. Anyway, he held her hand to his ear, and she just looked him in the eyes and whispered compassionately, "I'm so sorry your ear hurts." She remained with him, and Justin was able to ride through the wave of pain that day without the physical reactions he had been displaying.

How did a seventh-grade girl caught up in all the wrong things instinctively know how to work with a kid who confounded adults? Something about Justin drew the best out of Cory, and she was truly gifted in her ability to work with him.

Sadly, because of her awful home situation, Cory began to miss a lot of school. Last year, the counselor had a deal with her that she could keep coming to our class one period a day as long as she kept up her attendance. After a week of unexcused absences, though, she was told that she couldn't return to our class for two weeks. I made an appeal to the counselor, saying Cory shouldn't be deprived of the one positive thing she had going for her. I should have mentioned, too, that Justin didn't want to lose his friend, but I didn't think of that until later. The negative momentum had started, though, and perhaps because of a deteriorating home life, her attendance continued on a downward trajectory. Within a month she was transferred from Twin Oaks to a special school for students with emotional and behavioral needs.

That was a year ago, when Justin was in seventh grade. But I swear there are days this year when I see him staring at the door, and I think he is just waiting for Cory to walk in and start working alongside him like old times.

*   *   *   *

Another person needing further mention is my best buddy, Dallas. I give him a call as I'm packing my bag to head out of school after a long week.

"Hey! 'Sup, dude?" Dallas says with the greeting he has used since our middle-school days.

"Nothing much," I tell him, and I ask him if he wants to grab some food.

"Sorry, not today, Mikey. I got a babysitter for tonight. Cindy and I actually get to enjoy a date night that doesn't involve crying babies, broken sippy cups or oozing diapers. A sippy cup that opens up when it falls on the floor? Can you believe it? Isn't that the value of a sippy cup—that they're designed not to spill?"

I laugh and commiserate with him on the poor quality of sippy cups nowadays.

What's crazy about Dallas' story is that while I was studying in Boston, he met his wife, who was from Newton, a town outside of Boston, while they both were attending the University of Oregon. After they had their first child, they moved back to the east coast to be closer to her family. I still can't believe how lucky I am to have my old friend back in the same city again, just this time three thousand miles away from our old sixth-grade stomping grounds, where we used to have afterschool 7-Eleven Slurpee runs every Friday and weekend Nerf Gun wars.

We talk for a bit more, and I tell him, "No worries" that these last minute plans didn't work out. I keep forgetting that we're not seventeen anymore and I need to plan ahead to get on people's calendars. Dallas' life got substantially busier when they went from being a couple to a family of three after their nine-month old daughter, Abigail, entered the world.

"So what have you been up to this week, Dal?" I ask. "How has work been? You get any new video gigs?"

"Yeah, pretty much the same stuff," he says. "Some companies and clients that I make videos for are great, but others are just full of talking heads and execs who only care about the bottom line. But I can't complain—it's work. I do miss making videos that I was passionate about, though. There's just not a lot of money in the stories that need to be told the most, I guess."

Dallas always had the gift of communicating his thoughts well, and it definitely shines through in his videos. I really appreciate that about him. God knows how much his words have helped me process my own thoughts. "Sorry to hear, Dal. For what it's worth, I think your videos, even the corporate ones, have been pretty amazing. You've definitely got talent, man."

"No, things are good Mike—busy, but good. They really are." Dallas chuckles over the phone, as if to reassure me of his point, but the silence on the other end after his laugh makes me curious about what other thoughts might be running through his mind.

I decide to break up the silence and change the topic. "Hey, did you happen to watch any of the Patriots' Sunday Night Football game? Wait—I forgot who I was talking to. But did you at least hear about the controversial last call with the ref?"

Dallas laughs. "C'mon, Mikey, how long have I know you? I've never even pretended to care about sports."

"Not true!" I shoot back. "Remember when you first met Cindy and found out she was the only Jets fan from Boston? You started picking my brain so you wouldn't sound so clueless while talking to her on game day."

Dallas concedes, "Yeah, Cindy saw through that one pretty quickly."

I give Dallas a hard time, but I was just as guilty in college, slightly shifting my musical tastes and parts of my identity based on the girl I was trying to date. I know how quickly I went from weekend-Indie-concert-music guy to Russian-lit-reading guy. Not that I didn't like parts of those things before, during or after the pursuit of a particular girl, but no way would I have made it through *War and Peace* without a strong desire to impress a certain female Lit major, and let's just say I haven't listened to Radiohead's *Kid A* after I stopped dating Indie-Music Girl.

*   *   *   *

Other than Dallas, most of my other good friends from high school and college are in other states, and everyone's so busy we have just fallen out of touch. There's hardly much contact beyond the occasional Facebook message, birthday phone call, or quick catch-up if we happen to be in the same area. I think about friendship and how it's challenging to get to know people at my age, but having this social anxiety piece makes it that much harder. On an old *Seinfeld* episode, Jerry talked about this point exactly:

> When you're in your thirties, it's very hard to make a new friend. Whatever the group is that you've got now, that's who you're going with. You're not interviewing, you're not looking at any new people, you're not interested in seeing any applications. They don't know the places. They don't know the foods. They don't know the activities. If I meet a guy at a club, or a gym or someplace, I'm sure you're a very nice person, you seem to have a lot of potential, but we're just not hiring right now. Of course when you're a kid, you can be friends with anybody. Remember when you were a little kid, what were the qualifications? If someone's in front of my house *now*, that's my friend, they're my friend. That's it. Are you a grown-up? No. Great! Come on in. Let's jump up and down on my bed. And if you have anything in common at all, you like

Cherry Soda? I like Cherry Soda! We'll be best friends!

Seinfeld's bit makes me laugh, but it also feels uncomfortably true. I'm creeping up to my thirties, and I feel like *I* am the guy applying for a friend job. I'm not sure which came first—social anxiety, or the over-caring about each social interaction—because there are fewer opportunities to develop friendships. I'm sure they probably feed off each other. Either way, I feel like people just aren't hiring like they used to.

CHAPTER FIVE

I ENTER THE CLASSROOM literally seconds before Stevie strolls in with his distinctive gait that carries an extra beat of happiness. "Hiii, Miiister Sniiiff!"

"Hey, Stevie, how's it going? Good to see you this morning!"

Stevie responds with a huge smile and double-thumbs-up. I guess I get only one Mr. Sniff greeting today.

Justin comes running in, and I can see he is dysregulated. His senses, both input and output, are out of control. One strategy I was taught was to give some deep pressure in specific spots, which not only calms the student, but also gives them a better sense of their body and how it relates to the space around them. You might see a student with autism crawl into a tight space for the same effect. After giving Justin his final shoulder squeeze compression, I remind him to put his backpack away in the closet per his morning routine. Justin does a bouncy walk to the closet and starts to unload his books and lunch.

"How goes it this morning, Mr. Smith?" Jan asks as she walks in the door with her arms full of two grocery bags for this afternoon's Life Skills cooking lesson. Stephanie is behind her, mirroring her steps and hugging her own lunch bag in front of her.

"Good, Mrs. Jan. How are you doing today? It looks like you have a shadow this morning." I tilt my head toward Stephanie.

"It's funny, I noticed the same thing," Jan says. "Wherever I walk, my shadow seems to follow."

Stephanie looks up, and her expression changes from concentration to a smile. She is in on the joke now. "Look, Mr. Smith, every time! When I stop, my shadow stops."

Jan starts to walk, pauses, and then quickly begins to move forward again. Stephanie tries her best to keep up, but eventually breaks step and bursts into laughter. "Ohhhh, Mrs. Jan!" Stephanie giggles and speaks at the same time. I love the way our days start off.

The rest of our crew comes shuffling in. Molly is wearing black sweatpants and a purple zip-up GAP sweatshirt—the same outfit she wears every Wednesday. Following Molly is an unexpected guest—her father, Gary.

"Hello, Mr. Smith. How are you?" Gary asks with a friendly tone. "How's my Molly doing this week?"

"Very good! Molly has been a rock star as always!" I reply enthusiastically, but I can feel my heart starting to beat a little faster. "Have things been okay at home for Molly?"

"Well, actually that's why I wanted to check in with you. We've been seeing more behaviors—more refusals to eat, and let's just say none of us in the house are sleeping too well, with Moll waking up multiple times a night."

I'm trying to listen, but moisture is already lining my chest and back, and all I can do is hope that the dam of sweat isn't going to break out on my face next.

"She is also starting to do that nervous thing where she picks her lip again," Gary continues. "Is she doing that at school, too?"

I'm getting trapped in my own mind now. I hear what he is saying, but my brain is getting fuzzy and the conversation feels distant. "Oh, picking. No. I'm not sure. Jan, have you—I mean, did you notice anything this week?"

As the attention shifts to Jan, I try to get rid of the sweat now forming at the corners of my forehead, swiping it away with three of my fingers. Jan is answering, and I'm trying to remind myself of what Tim has told me: *It's okay. People don't notice, or if they do, they don't care.* Jan's response is finished, and the conversation turns back to me.

Molly's father adds, "My wife and I were brainstorming, and we really haven't changed her routine. Actually, before this last rough stretch she—"

Drops are forming and now sliding down my warm cheeks. I can hear myself answering at the appropriate times, but only thirty percent of my mind is actually in the conversation.

"Yes, well, that's good there were positives before that . . . "

"Maybe it's just a phase, and it will return back to where she was at before . . ."

"Is she going to the bathroom at home? She hasn't gone in a while here."

Sweat is now starting to fall from my face and making blotches on my dark blue shirt. I try to engage back in the conversation. "I'll keep looking for any changes in Molly's behavior for sure." I look at Molly's dad, and I can only imagine what he is thinking. I don't give him the chance to ask the obvious "Are you all right?" question. I've got to end this discussion quickly and get to a bathroom. "Sorry, I have to go the restroom, Gary, but I'll write a note about it and put it in her binder and let you know."

"Thanks, Mr. Smith, I appreciate it." I hear the words fading as I am already halfway to the bathroom, located near the back of our class. To my embarrassment, in my quest to escape, I've failed to say goodbye to Molly's dad and abandoned the courtesy of walking him to the door.

Once inside the bathroom, I turn the blue C to full strength. I cup my hands together and douse my face with the soothing, saving water. On my final splash, I hold my hands over my face and take in three deep breaths. I try to remind myself of what Tim said: *Escape to a safe place. Regain composure. It's going to be okay.* I feel my internal temperature decrease slightly. The sweating has slowed, and the fuzzyheaded feeling is starting to fade, but the negative assessment of the interaction is just now beginning. I turn off the cool water, wishing this morning could have simply ended with the lighthearted moment of Stephanie shadowing Jan.

*   *   *   *

Our class goes through morning meeting, reading, snack, math, and then Barb and Jan take the students to the cafeteria for lunch. I remind them of Molly's decreased appetite at home and ask them to monitor how lunch goes today. As I start to pull out my peanut butter sandwich and take my lunch break in front of the computer screen, the phone rings.

"Hello? Oh, yes, Mr. Ballamy, I'll come by right now." Interesting. I wonder why the principal wants to see me midday. It's not unheard of to meet with your boss during the workday, but Mr. Ballamy is not the warmest of individuals, and if he calls you to his office, it's probably not for a pat on the back. Other teachers have nicknamed him "The General" because of his tough, no-nonsense demeanor. I always thought that it was a fitting title, too, with the pronunciation of "Ball-a-my" sounding a whole lot like "Fol-low me."

To be honest, my relationship with Mr. Ballamy hasn't been the best since I started at Twin Oaks. He's not a bad guy, but I know our kids are not at the forefront of his mind. For example, last October, during my first year of teaching, all students and staff in the school received shirts with the Twin Oaks logo and 2011-2012 printed on them. When I went to the front office and asked about the best way to get our students their T-shirts, Jill, our head secretary, said with an embarrassed tone, "I'm sorry, Michael, I don't think Mr. Ballamy ordered any for the Special Education kids." Jill went on to assure me that we could have any leftover shirts. I passed. I don't think Stevie or Molly would fit in the unclaimed XXL shirts anyways. For the rest of that month I had a hard time not thinking about those T-shirts every time I saw Mr. Ballamy.

*   *   *   *

"Michael, come on in," Mr. Ballamy says with his deep, authoritative voice. He wears a bright red sweater that looks as if it was borrowed from Bobby Knight's closet. The principal's eyes stay fixed on the paperwork spread out before him on his desk cluttered with papers and sticky-note telephone messages.

"Hello, Mr. Ballamy, how are you?" For some reason I still can't seem to call him Frank as many teachers do. I think it's partially an age thing. I still feel like anyone forty and above are the true adults, and I'm the fairly-recent postbac grad pretending to be an adult.

"How are the students doing?" he asks. "Any complaints from parents?"

"No, the kids and the class are all doing great. Kind of funny, the other day—"

I get cut off as Mr. Ballamy starts in with the reason for my summons—"Glad to hear that, Michael. Well, I called you in because we are adding a new student to your class. The people at the district office say this particular case could be rather challenging and intense. The student apparently once was normal."

There is that word *normal* that I loathe, implying that our kids are *abnormal.* Now isn't the time for a delicate discussion with the boss on a more sensitive choice of words, though, so I say nothing.

"She used to go to another middle school in the district," Mr. Ballamy continues, "but she got stung by a bee, and had a life-threatening allergic reaction. Now she is in a wheelchair and can no longer speak. I think she just kind of sits there. Terrible situation."

"Oh, my gosh . . . how awful. I'm so sorry to hear about that."

"The worst part, Michael, is that mom is a lawyer, and she almost took our district to court earlier this school year. It sounds like she wasn't too happy with what her previous school, Woodland Middle, was offering in terms of services and the type of classroom she would be in. I heard from their principal that they had a couple of five-hour meetings that didn't lead to any real progress. Sounds like she could be some real trouble."

I nod as Mr. Ballamy expounds more on the situation, but then I realize I had forgotten to ask the most important question. "Mr. Ballamy, what is her name?"

"Her name? Oh It's Emily . . . Emily Thompkins. Here's her file." He pulls out a file much smaller than I am used to seeing for students in my classroom. Most of my kids have been receiving services since they were preschoolers, or even earlier, but Emily has been in Special Education for less than a year. Suddenly, the thinness of her file makes me sad.

*   *   *   *

As I walk back to my class, I open Emily's file and begin to scan the Special Ed paperwork. A warm voice hails me from behind and breaks my concentration—

"Hey, Michael!"

It's Josie Liu, one of our eighth-grade Language Arts teachers, who started to teach at Twin Oaks the same year as me. Josie has an even-tempered disposition and can come across as slightly serious at first. As you get to know her, though, more of her personality and sense of humor is revealed. She is very smart and funny with her observational comments. You might say or do something silly or comical, and some time in the future she will refer back to it at the perfect moment to bring the joke home.

"Hey Josie, how's it going?" I ask as I return her smile. Actually, I seem to break out into a grin whenever I'm around her. "You ready for the *five*?" I tuck Emily's file under my left arm and take a step in her direction.

Josie has a small-mouthed smile, which rises slightly on the left side. "Ready when you are." Without hesitation we both raise our right hands high in the air and connect with a strong high-five at the top of Josie's arm length. We then follow through with a downward swinging arm motion, connecting a second time for a backwards low-five.

—CLAP—CLAP—

This full-circle double slap we pull off to perfection was made famous by one of the classic movies I grew up on. "Another successful *Top Gun* high-five! Well done by you, Ms. Liu."

"Not bad, considering I've never seen the movie, right? Hey, it's only taken me until February to get this *five* down." I wag my head in mock disbelief that Josie still hasn't seen *Top Gun*.

She pretends to ignore me and asks, "Why were you walking around with your head down like that? I'm worried you're going to take out one of the poor sixth-graders if you're not watching where you're going."

I produce the file folder to justify my obliviousness while walking. Her previous comment does spark an embarrassing memory from elementary school, however. Even though my stories are not skillfully told, or usually all that captivating, Josie always seems interested in hearing them. "Did I tell you, Ms. Liu, that when I was in fourth grade I wasn't paying attention and ran into my teacher while playing basketball at recess? I literally sent the poor lady flying."

"That's horrible," she says, shaking her head. "I'm pretty sure that would only happen to you, Michael."

"Yeah, the worst part was, she was older and kind of frail, and she ended up having to go to the hospital. I felt terrible and almost cried in front of my classmates that day. The kids made fun of me, and even the teacher teased me about it—after she was able to return to school a few days later."

Josie laughs quietly and smiles along with my story. I like her laugh. It's faint, and you could almost miss it if you weren't looking for it. I've noticed she is a little more selective with her laugh, so if I do say something that elicits one, I feel an extra sense of pride.

"I haven't heard the sending-the-teacher-to-the-hospital story, Michael," she says. "Next lunchtime you should come to the teachers' lounge, and you can give me more details about this scarring event from your childhood."

"Uh, I think that's pretty much the whole story," I say, but then pause, realizing her comment was really an invitation to eat and connect with the teachers more. "Yeah, I keep meaning to eat lunch with you guys. I've just been busy lately, but I will make it to the staff lounge some time."

I know the busy part is only half-true. The thing holding me back is not the work that needs to be done, but worrying about eye contact and sweating. While I want to be social again, whenever I weigh the pros and cons, I decide it isn't worth it.

I try to return to a comment from earlier in the conversation: "Aren't *you* ever worried about these kids coming through here, Ms. Liu? Some of these eighth-graders look like they're growing mustaches and could run you over pretty easily. No offense, Ms. Liu . . . it's not that you are small. Well, no, I guess it is because you *are* pretty small."

Josie socks my upper arm playfully and says, "I pack a big punch for someone my size! I was voted 'Most Likely to Become a Sports Star' back in high school."

"Really?" I say with true surprise.

"No, not at all—but I do appreciate the confidence you have in my athletic abilities," she replies drily.

My mind flashes back to my pre-anxiety days and being voted "Most Social Male" in high school. Boy, that seems like a lifetime ago now.

"Anyways, Michael, change of topic. I was thinking about your kiddos the other day. It's been a while since I've seen any of them lately. How is my friend Stevie doing? I used to see him all the time during passing period, but I think our schedules are off now. I miss how he used to say, 'Hiii Ms. Liuuuu,' whenever he would see me."

I can easily picture the scene. Ms. Liu is very comfortable with, and cares about, all of the students in my classroom. She does have an affinity for Stevie, though. "Yeah, Stevie is still the head of our welcoming committee. He's doing great! I'm sure he misses seeing you too."

"Some of the peer tutors from my fifth period class, Chelsea and Rosa, told me that Devonte's birthday is coming up? Is that true? Do you guys have big plans?"

"Well, party planning was never really my specialty, but it would be cool if you're able to send a few extra peer tutors that day so we can celebrate our Number One Baseball Fan's birthday."

"Definitely!' Josie says enthusiastically. I smile widely as I look into her eyes, which curiously don't freak me out like most eyes do.

RINGRING**RING**

"Well, better head back. Probably shouldn't be late to my own class, since I just gave the kids a lecture the other day about being on time."

"Yep, guess I better go too. Okay, well, keep me posted on Devonte's birthday celebration. I know my kids would love to help." I thank Josie.

"One more for the road?" she asks with a slight hesitation.

—CLAP—CLAP—

*   *   *   *

Some of the best advice I received when going through my Master's program was to find and connect with General Education teachers who are passionate about including students with special needs into the culture of your school. Last year, as first-year teachers, Ms. Liu and I met during orientation, and she seemed very interested in she and her kids forming those relationships with my students. Josie became that bridge they talked about in my Special Ed teaching courses. Before Winter Break of that first year, she had already established an application process and schedule for students who wanted to come into my class to build friendships and act as helpers for our students.

During one of our pre-staff meeting conversations, we came up with the idea of changing the title of those who volunteered from "helpers" to "peer tutors." I think, as an English teacher, Josie said it best: "It may just seem like semantics, but titles matter. We don't want kids from my class coming in thinking they are just *helping* those who are in need. Everyone who comes into your classroom is not only often equal in age, but they're also equal in importance. They need to remember they are peers and friends, first and foremost." I was blown away by her thoughtful perspective, and from that point forward we went with "peer tutors."

It kills me to have met Josie, see her caring heart, and gotten to know her witty sense of humor, only to find out that she is in a long-term, long-distance relationship with a guy from college. He seems like a nice person from all her stories and descriptions, but man, I hope that guy knows how lucky he is and appreciates all her amazing qualities. She volunteers working with elderly folks on weekends, for crying out loud!

I walk back to the classroom, smiling and recharged, ready to go for the second half of the day. The morning of profuse sweating is practically a distant memory—good thing, too, because I hear Barb shout to Jan from the bathroom, "You know, I'm not sure we have a spare change of clothes for Stevie this time . . . looks like it's going to get messy!"

Uh-oh. I know the drill, and go running for the gloves and antibacterial wipes.

CHAPTER SIX

I SLAP MY ALARM as the first round of annoying beeps goes off. Why did I stay up so late watching Monday Night Football? I knew that once I started watching I wouldn't be able to go to bed until after midnight. Man, the west coasters don't know how good they have it for sports-viewing. They can watch a whole game and still go to bed by nine-thirty.

I roll over and glare at the appalling bright red '4:45' on my clock. I stumble around my apartment, half-awake, trying to get ready. I throw my teacher clothes into my gym bag and head out the door.

           *   *   *   *

I realize that basketball, for someone with social anxieties, is the ultimate blessing in disguise. As my thoughts start to race and the sweat starts to pour, I force myself to remember that I am playing freakin' basketball and it would be weird not to be sweating at this time. This one actually works almost every time, and for those forty-five minutes I do regain a sense of my old self. The after-game conversations, where I am sweating more than I did when I was on the court, are a different story, but at this point I'll take close to an hour of mind-respite every time.

The game itself was good competition. I played in high school, so I have some skills, and, although my athleticism is eroding each year, I still find a way to contribute to the team in one way or another. I find that there are two distinct types of people who do surprisingly well in our pick-up basketball games.

Type 1 is the old man who has lost his quick moves, but who practices and perfects one skill—the ability to shoot. Our fifty-five-year-old science teacher, Larry Gill, is like that. It's cool, because every time he hits a three, someone will shout out, "Larry the Legend!" If the guy was thirty years younger and a little more athletic, I think he could honestly help the Celtics win another championship. I know for a fact he would outshoot Rondo.

Type 2 is the overly physical former-football-player guy. Mr. Jones, the gym teacher, has a little of that in him. Even though I have played organized basketball almost my entire life, and pretty much every day until college, Mr. Jones takes me to school like no one's business. The seeming lack of caring what a foul is can be quite advantageous in these games. He'll lower his shoulder and go strong to the hole, and, I'll be honest—I don't have the guts to take a charge from a guy who outweighs me by seventy pounds.

I hold my own that day—hit a couple of threes and make a few smart passes—you know, the typical past-his-prime, but still-somewhat-competent stuff. It's fun, though, and definitely starts my day off on the right foot. High-fives are given all around as we mutually decide that game number three would have to end in a tie with only twenty minutes left to shower, change, and get ready for the school day.

*   *   *   *

Devonte is in sixth grade and on the autism spectrum. He is a sharp dresser, and his dark hair is always neatly trimmed. Although he's a little on the shorter, stockier side, when he moves on to seventh and then eighth grade, I think he will continue to grow and have an athletic build to match his enthusiasm for sports. Devonte is also our highest functioning student. He picks up concepts faster than his classmates, but most of his academic skills are probably around a kindergarten/first-grade level.

I know one of the big Hollywood misperceptions is that, if you are a person with autism, then you have a Rain Man-like ability to count cards or dropped toothpicks on the floor at a surreal speed. That isn't the case for Justin, Molly, or even Garret, who moved up to high school last year, but it is somewhat true for Devonte. He doesn't count tiles on the ceiling or memorize famous dates in American history, but he has an unbelievable memory for baseball facts and statistics. It's strange, because he will sometimes forget that $10 + 7 = 17$, but if you ask him about a Red Sox statistic from the mid-1980s through the current day, he will be able to retrieve that information with astonishing speed and accuracy.

He is shy in general—not one to speak more than a short sentence or two to anybody, unless it's on the topic of baseball. Devonte's speech is also interesting, as he will switch mid-sentence from a monotone, lower-register voice to a higher-pitched one. I often wonder what goes on with him whenever this change occurs.

On this Friday, Devonte comes into the classroom, wearing what I'm assuming is a prized birthday present. "Devonte, that is awesome!" I tell him. "Did you get that jersey this morning? Happy birthday, buddy!"

"Yes," he says proudly. "It is a Curt Shilling jersey." Sure enough, he switches to his lower register. "Career stats: 3,116 strikeouts, 216 wins."

"Thanks, Devonte, I didn't know that. Did you learn those stats while you were you playing an old video game?" I ask with sincere curiosity.

"Baseball cards. Curt Schilling played for the Baltimore Orioles, 1988; Houston Astros, 1991; Philadelphia Phillies, 1992; Arizona"—he changes to a tenor—"Diamondbacks, 2000; Boston Red Sox, 2004."

"Wow, good info, Devonte. I didn't know he had such a long career. I actually thought he started with Philadelphia."

"No, he started with Baltimore Orioles, 1988; Houston Astros, 1991; Philadelphia Phil..."

I gently cut him off so he doesn't go through the whole list again. I feel bad after doing this, especially since I'm trying to encourage him to talk more with others. "Devonte, was Curt Schilling the 2001 World Series' Most Valuable Player when playing with the Diamondbacks?"

"Yes," Devonte answers, seeming happy enough with the baseball facts he has dispensed for the day. I remember that series against the Yankees in 2001, but the one I will always associate Schilling with is the classic "bloody sock game" in 2004 that led to Boston's first World Series championship in 86 years. It was the series that changed the Boston sports fans' psyche forever.

As Devonte turns to put his backpack away, Chelsea, Rosa, and Brandon from Ms. Liu's class come in with a giant card made out of white butcher paper in the shape of a baseball that has been signed by all her students. They start singing "Happy Birthday" loudly and with gusto. These kind-hearted kids have no idea what is coming next.

A blood-curdling scream breaks out that freezes the festive song in its tracks. Molly begins to bang the desk with her forearm, stomp her feet, and wail. Unexpected noises can always be hard for her, but something about that particular song has hit a nerve for some reason.

"Hey, Barbara," I say, "I need some papers picked up in the office. Would you and Molly be able to help us out and grab them?"

Barbara knows that is code for taking Molly on a calming break. Barbara taps Molly on the elbow and says, "Come on, hon'."

Molly does something surprising, though—she says, "No." Hmmm . . . that was a first-time response. She loves to walk for a break, especially when that walk means getting out of a stressful situation.

Barbara tries to reassure her and encourages her to stand.

"No," Molly says again in a somewhat wobbly voice.

I ask the kids from the classroom if it is okay if we pause the singing for just one second. I kneel down next to Molly and ask if she wants to stay.

"Yes," she replies softly.

"Okay, Molly, but I think the kids are going to finish singing 'Happy Birthday' to Devonte. Will you be able to stay for that?"

"Yes."

"Okay, guys, thanks for being patient. Maybe we can finish the song at this level voice." I model a volume close to a whisper. The kids signal their understanding, and are much more perceptive of what just happened than I would have been as a middle school student.

The kids proceed, "Happy birthday to you..." Molly is wringing her hands and starting to make vocalizations of anxiety.

"Happy birthday, dear Devonte . . ." Molly is tightly squeezing her hands and rocking back and forth with a few short foot stomps. She doesn't scream, though, and as hard as it clearly is for her, she stays for the whole song.

"Happy birthday to youuu!" The song has ended, and the kids had kept it at the perfect volume. Then, out of nowhere, a small, high-pitched voice you would miss were it not quiet in that moment goes "to you" a second after the song finishes. Molly repeats the last couple of words and is rocking back and forth still, this time with a huge smile on her face.

The kids give Devonte the jumbo-sized card and bring out mini-cupcake treats for all of the students. I walk over to Devonte and give him a fist-bump. "Happy birthday, Devonte! That was pretty neat that Molly sang for you. That is the first time I've ever heard her sing that song."

Devonte continues to focus on the royal blue frosting of his cupcake, but says, "Yes," in a squeaky voice. I do believe that part of him understands that it wasn't easy for Molly to celebrate with the others, just as sometimes it can be challenging for him to carry on long conversations. Molly made it through the song for him, though. I look at Devonte and his jersey and think, *Curt Schilling and his brave bloody sock performance doesn't have anything on our kids and what they accomplish all the time. We Special Education teachers just happen to be the lucky ones who get to see it.*

CHAPTER SEVEN

THE SLURPING SOUNDS OF the suction device reminds me of having my teeth cleaned in a dentist's chair. Nurse Nancy is going through her routine of clearing out the saliva and phlegm that is starting to build up in Emily's mouth, and she skillfully clears what Emily is no longer able to swallow. We are all thankful that Nurse Nancy, who has been assigned to Emily full-time for the rest of the year, is such a natural addition to our team.

The dynamics of the room have shifted this first week since Emily has arrived. One student that has taken an instant liking to Emily is Molly. She will often get up and hover near Emily's wheelchair, rocking back and forth with a tranquil look on her face. Nancy will usually ask Molly if she wants to say "hi" to Emily. Originally Molly was content just being in proximity to Emily, but now she is saying "yes," and after a little rehearsal in her mind will say "hi" in her gentle, high-pitched voice.

"That is very sweet of you Molly," Nancy tells her. The nurse helps Emily lift her head up, because her neck is no longer strong enough to support her head upright for long periods of time. One time after Molly greets her, Emily holds her head up and looks Molly directly in the eyes. I am starting to wonder if there is more going on cognitively than she is able to express.

"I think Emily is saying 'hi' back to you, Molly. You want to give her a high-five?" Nancy gently turns Emily's arm and supports it so her right palm faces upwards in Molly's direction. Molly, who has always shown a strong aversion to touch due to her autism, surprises us by bending at the hip slightly and slowly reaching toward Emily. Her feet stay planted, but she approaches Emily's outstretched hand like a child tentatively reaching toward a fresh-out-of-the-oven cookie, unsure whether she should touch it or not. Molly gets within three inches of Emily's hand, and then snaps her fingers forward for a quick touch before pulling them back again. Molly smiles slightly and rocks as she makes her way back to her chair to continue her morning routine.

Nancy, Jan, Barbara, and I look at each other, impressed with Molly's progress. Although Stevie has broken through and gotten a morning high-five from Molly with his persistence, this is the first time I've seen Molly initiate touch since coming here. I've been trying to get that elusive high-five since Day One, and have still not been successful.

"Way to go, Molly!" Jan shouts from across the room, pumping her fist in the air. Devonte is working with her on letters and is clearly confused by this exuberant outburst.

*   *   *   *

Today is my first meeting with Emily's mom, Ms. Thompkins. I know that Mr. Ballamy and she have already talked about the logistical aspects of Emily joining Twin Oaks, the safety concerns, and the nurse's role in her care. I am somewhat curious and concerned about the legal issues at the previous school, but at the same time I think sometimes it's better not to know all the details and have a fresh start.

The meeting is scheduled for eleven o'clock. I planned to take my fast-acting anxiety medication at ten-thirty, but I realize in a panic I have forgotten to bring it school. *Oh, crap!* I think as I make sure the kids are covered and then slip into our classroom bathroom. My forehead starts to radiate with that familiar, unwelcomed warmth. I grab a paper towel and put it under the faucet. I hold the cold towel to my face for a good ten seconds, and go back to what Tim has taught me about deep breathing and giving myself positive messages: *Breathe in....2..3....hold...2...3....out through the mouth...2...3...*

I go through this process a few more times and remind myself of the calming phrases that Pastor Tim taught me last week, "It's going to be fine. It's always fine. And if it's not, I can always retreat." I leave the bathroom, uncomfortable and with scattered attention, but hoping to focus on our conversation about Emily without getting lost in my own thoughts.

*   *   *   *

As I enter the conference room in the office, I see Ms. Thompkins already seated with her black power suit, subtly conveying she is in charge of this meeting. In front of her is a binder containing Emily's evaluation reports and a hefty Individualized Education Program, which outlines a student's present levels and the goals, accommodations, modifications and support services necessary to meet those goals. A legal notepad is positioned to Ms. Thompkins' right, ready to document our conversation.

She stands to shake my hand. "Hello, Mr. Smith, I'm Rachael Thompkins. I'm assuming you've already heard some negative reports about me, but I'm here for one reason alone, and that is to make sure Emily is safe and gets everything that she is entitled to by law." There is a toughness in her voice that matches her firm handshake.

I fumble a little bit with my greeting, but I am able to let her know how successful this first week has been with integrating Emily into the classroom. "I hope you believe me, Ms. Thompkins, when I say that my goal is to make sure that Emily is safe, and that we will work as hard as possible to provide the right environment to help her meet her goals and objectives. I'm also a huge believer in clear communication between school and home."

Ms. Thompkins doesn't smile, but seems to be taking in what I've said. The pause in the action, however, allows my anxious brain to kick in. It was fine when our initial encounter almost stunned me, but now that the anxiety ball is rolling, the first beads of sweat are forming around the corners of my hairline. My mind is getting that dizzy, swimmy feeling. I try to recall specific examples of positive moments, but half my mind is monitoring my sweating, while the other half is thinking about how much eye contact I should be giving to Ms. Thompkins.

It doesn't appear, however, that Ms. Thompkins notices the sweat now forming across my face and forearms—at least not yet. "Well, that is good to hear, Mr. Smith." I can hear slightly less distrust in her voice. "I take it that you read her file and know about the whole incident."

Since I am now dripping with sweat, I have a hard time keeping my head up while talking to Ms. Thompkins, so I keep my eyes down and nod. "Yes, it must have been horrible for you. I'm so sorry that happened. How long was it before 911 was called after the allergic reaction?"

"Almost five minutes after what we are pretty convinced was a bee sting—five minutes of oxygen loss that changed her whole life. Who knows how different things could have been if I had known how allergic she really was, or if Em had had an EpiPen that day."

Just the way Ms. Thompkins calls her daughter "Em" disarms me even more, and I realize in that moment that there is no way I can feel anything negative toward this mother, who has already been through so much. My thoughts drift as I picture the hives sprouting all over Emily's body and her desperately trying to breathe. Ms. Thompkins brings me back to the present when she says, "Uh, Mr. Smith, are you okay? You seem to be sweating a lot."

I look up, feeling shame at the question I equally hate and fear. "Sorry, sorry," I stammer, "I just, uh, haven't been feeling great. Could you excuse me for a moment?"

Ms. Thompkins gives a wide-eyed nod, communicating, Yes, please, that would be good for everyone.

I retreat into the restroom. Frustrated with myself, I want to shout out loud to my nemesis—*C'mon, give me a break! Freakin' Anxiety! Can't I have one important conversation without you showing up and ruining everything?!* Although this conversation is happening only in my mind, the venting feels good, and the anger supersedes my anxiety for that moment. As I stand in front of the sink, splashing my face with cold water, I begin to feel calmer, although I'm not sure if it's my exasperation or the retreat to the restroom that is helping me feel this way. My brain gets a tingling sensation, almost as if my body recognizes that the adrenaline rush has come and gone and my fight-or-flight reflexes can rest. I have also learned that prickly feeling in my brain is a sign that I will be able to remain calm for the rest of the conversation with Ms. Thompkins.

I apologize again when I return, even though she probably doesn't know whether I am apologizing for my profuse sweating or my quick exit. Ms. Thompkins has a softer tone, as she continues speaking. "So, yes, I just want to make sure that everything is in order for my girl. It sounds like it was a good first week, which is a tremendous relief." She gives a tentative smile, her first of the meeting, which makes me feel better. "I just want for her, number one, to always be safe, and, number two, to be in a place where she will still make gains as a student. Even if I don't know what that progress will actually look like, I don't want one bee-sting to be the end of all things good for my daughter."

My heart breaks with her fear of all good things ending for her child. I look Ms. Thompkins in the eye and say with sincerity, "First of all, thank you for sharing about something that I'm sure is very difficult to talk about."

She nods slowly.

"I just want to assure you that Emily is coming into a very supportive and caring environment," I continue. "It's the whole staff—Barb, Jan, our specialists, myself, and now Nurse Nancy. We really work great together as a team. Her classmates, too, are amazing kids." I pause, my mind focused on the conversation, not my sweat levels. "I truly believe that Emily is in the right spot. She has already started connecting with her classmates and bringing some of them out of their shells."

I love these moments of being myself again. I feel confident in what I am saying.

Ms. Thompkins also seems pleased with our conversation. "Well, thank you, Mr. Smith. I think we understand each other. I just want the best for Em."

We all stand, and the meeting comes to a close with handshakes. Even though only twenty minutes have passed, I now know what kind of parent Ms. Thompkins is, and she definitely is not scary or unreasonable as Mr. Ballamy led me to believe. One thing without question is that Ms. Thompkins' end goal is, and has always been, her daughter's well-being, and parents with that perspective are ones I will always respect.

*   *   *   *

Sometimes, when I can't sleep, I eventually get out of bed and read. Last Friday's conversation with Ms. Thompkins about Emily is still on my mind. *How incomprehensible is it to go from being a typical seventh-grader worried about boys and learning pre-algebra to not being able to do anything by yourself again because you are imprisoned in your body?*

I stare at the ceiling. After fifteen minutes I know I am not going to fall asleep in this state, so I get up and look for the book *Adam* I started a while back but never finished. The author is a priest named Henri Nouwen. Even though I no longer attend church, I have always been fascinated by his story—a priest, and well-respected author, who suddenly felt called to leave his position and work at a center for adults with special needs.

Sitting on my living room chair, I read from this book Nouwen was working on before he passed away. He shares about Adam, a man at the center with severe disabilities, whom he has worked with and befriended. I am struck by the way Nouwen describes Adam—not only the way he thinks about him, but also the way he believes God saw him. The quote that sticks out to me tonight about Adam is that he was:

> Precious, beloved, whole, and born of God.
> Adam bore silent witness to this mystery, which has nothing to do with whether or not he could speak, walk, or express himself, whether or not he made money, had a job, was fashionable, famous, married or single . . . Unfortunately, there is a very loud, consistent, and powerful message coming to us from our world that leads us to believe that we must prove our belovedness by how we look, by what we have, and by what we can accomplish. We become preoccupied with 'making it' in this life.

I sit with that thought for a while. Each one of the kids I get to work with adds so much to the lives of those who get to know them. To be honest, sometimes I don't even recognize these gifts being passed out as I get sucked up in the busy world of teaching, paperwork, meetings, and, of course, my own self-conscious mind. I am still saddened, thinking about Emily's story and how she and her family now have a new, unimaginably challenging life, but I am thankful that we are the ones who can work with her now. I read those words one last time—"precious, beloved, whole, and born of

God." A sudden wave of tiredness finally comes over me. I drag myself to bed, close my eyes, and slip into my first peaceful sleep in weeks.

CHAPTER EIGHT

IT'S NOT JUST MOLLY who has connected with Emily through daily high-fives; Stephanie and Emily have also become very close. Whenever we go out to the lunchroom, computer lab, or gym, Stephanie is always the one who wants to help push Emily's wheelchair. She is also a natural with being able to carry on a "conversation" with "Emmy," as she calls her. Stephanie shows none of the discomfort adults display when trying to carry on a reciprocal conversation with someone who doesn't speak. In fact, I credit Stephanie with leading us to the biggest breakthrough with Emily.

Stephanie is the greatest One Direction fan I have ever met. You can tell she is in a good mood when she belts out, "That's what makes you beautiful!" loud and proud, in her slightly monotone voice. At the beginning of the year she wrote a letter, with adult support, to the English-Irish pop stars to motivate her to do some writing. Though they didn't answer her questions, they did send back a signed 8x10 of the band. Stephanie's mom said she has it hung up in her room and says "goodnight" to each member of the band before going to sleep.

Her love of One Direction is so strong she would happily steer every conversation back to "my guys," as she likes to call them. We actually have to limit how many times she can talk about the band. It sounds harsh, but I think three conversations a day still ends up feeling like a lot of One

Direction. That doesn't include the music videos she earns for completing a certain number of tasks.

The room has a certain buzz today, with all of the kids working hard on a variety of assignments. Pam, our assistive technology (AT) specialist, has come in for the afternoon to trial a couple of different device options with Justin. She hopes to find a device that will help him better express his wants and needs. Barbara is leading a small group with Molly and Devonte on identifying the characters and setting from a *Matt and Molly* lesson. These are very short, highly visual stories written to help students with autism develop linguistic and social skills. Our Molly always seems to get a kick out of the name connection. One of our peer tutors, Chelsea, is reading from the *Twilight* series to Emily. Ms. Thompkins shared in one of our daily correspondences that Emily used to love reading those books before the accident. Jan is trying to work with Stevie, who is expressing his strong desire not to practice letter sounds by putting his head down on the table.

It is during Stephanie's video reward time that she asks if Emily can join her. We agree, of course, and put the *Twilight* reading on hold, and Chelsea helps wheel Emily over to the computers with Stephanie. I load the page of music videos and am about to click on her favorite "What Makes You Beautiful" song, when Stephanie holds up both hands and yells, "Stop!"

I'm taken aback. "Why Stephanie? What's up? You want to pick a different song?"

In her low voice and halting speech she says, "No, Mr. Smith. I told Emmy this morning she could choose." As I am thinking about how I can support Emily to "make a choice,"

Stephanie says something astonishing: "Emmy, you tell me which one you like, okay?"

Stephanie can read only about twelve sight words consistently, but she knows these videos from their YouTube thumbnails like the back of her hand. She reads the first choice: "Emmy, first is 'Beautiful.' I sing that one a lot." Then she does something very smart—she pauses, pauses some more, keeps pausing, and eventually says, "Okay, you want a new song."

I am so impressed that she does something we as adults have a very difficult time doing—giving kids the chance to answer. I know Stephanie understands that Emily doesn't respond verbally like the other kids, but she gives her time, as if waiting for a reply. That's when Stephanie's questions, and the presence of our AT specialist, sets off a light bulb in my own mind.

"Stephanie, you are a genius!" I exclaim. "Can you wait for one second? Let's see if we can help Emily answer your question."

*   *   *   *

Stephanie showed us that we were not asking Emily the right type of questions, and more importantly, not providing a way for her to answer them. We were talking *at* her, not giving her the opportunity to respond.

"Hey, Pam!" I call out while racing to the other side of the room. "You got a second for an idea?"

Pam gets filled in on the plan, finishes with Justin, and in less than five minutes rigs up a little communication system from the bag of devices she brought along as part of her assistive technology trial for Justin. To the back handle of Emily's chair Pam attaches a metal arm ending in a three-pronged grip that can hold a communication device, which she calls a *Big Mac* button. I've learned about these devices in grad school, but this world of assistive technology is new to me as a second-year teacher. I observe Pam closely and take it all in.

"This is a fairly simple device where we can program in one previously recorded response at a time," Pam says. "See, if you hold down this side switch like this, then we can give Emily a way to express a thought by hitting the main button when she wants that phrase to be spoken." Pam holds down 'Record' on the side of the *Big Mac* until a light turns red, and then speaks into the machine, "Stephanie, that's the song I want." She hits the *Big Mac,* and we hear her recorded phrase. This will be a good way to test, if given a basic device, whether or not Emily is able to communicate a preference.

After the message is recorded and the button is attached to the end of the arm, it is locked in place about two inches to the right of Emily's head. In fact, if Emily sneezed, her body would probably move enough to hit the switch. Pam gets down on a knee to be at eye-level with Emily.

"Hi Emily," she says. "My name is Pam." The AT specialist speaks slowly, allowing Emily time to process her words. "We are going to try something new. Your friend Stephanie really wants to know which song you want to listen to right now. We'll give you three choices. If you move your head, it will hit a button that will let us know which song you want." Pam rubs the right side of Emily's head to show where she would be making contact with the *Big Mac.* "Just move your head like this, okay, sweetheart?" Pam gives Emily a little bit of pressure from the left side so Emily's right temple connects with the button and we hear, "Stephanie, that's the song I want."

"Very good, Emily," Pam reinforces with a soft, warm voice. "Now let's see if you can do it all on your own. Do you want to give it a try and hit the button right here?" Unlike most of our conversations with Emily in which we talk and talk, now we just wait and watch. Five seconds, ten seconds, fifteen seconds . . . nothing happens. "That's okay, Emily—let's just give this a try."

Pam asks Stephanie if she still wants to give Emily a chance to pick a song, but she warns, "Emily may just be getting tired."

You can see Stephanie's excitement to hear her friend's new "voice" though, and she encourages Emily, "C'mon, Emmy. Try to talk, okay?"

I smile at Stephanie's eager prompting.

Stephanie starts off with the first choice: "This is 'One Thing.' It is a very good song." Like a veteran educator, Stephanie does the hardest thing—she just waits. Again, though, nothing happens. After thirty seconds, we ask Stephanie to try another one. "Emmy, I like this song, 'Gotta Be You.' You want this?" No movement again. Emily's eyes are alert, but between how difficult it is to keep her head up, let alone move her head purposefully, I am starting to see a failed outcome to this trial. I have found that we never want to set low expectations for our students, because we may miss out on some of their biggest accomplishments. At the same time, though, there is a point when you just have to accept that a student, or even you, might not be capable of something. Is that quitting, or having realistic expectations?

Either way, I am proud of Stephanie for her desire to want to connect with her new friend better.

"Thanks, Stephanie, that was great," Pam says. "Do you want to maybe just pick one of those songs for Emily?"

I turn toward Pam to thank her for her help, but Stephanie quickly insists, "We told Emmy three choices. She only got two." I smile and let her know she had a good point, and we should try one more. Stephanie beams and moves her body up a little bit from her slouched position to look Emily in the eyes. "Emmy, you want the 'Beautiful' song?" She pauses, and nothing happens. Although some would say that we were unsuccessful, I had to think that the whole process was quite the win. Not only did Stephanie kick-start the whole idea, but she also showed us as adults to think outside of the box with Emily. I was super proud of the way—

"Stephanie, that's the one I want." My thoughts are interrupted by Pam's recorded voice. Our heads all shoot over to Emily's chair to see who has pushed the button. No one else is around. We all stare at Emily. She is grimacing, as if she had strained every muscle in her body to move her head those two inches to hit that switch.

My breath stops. "Emily, can you say that one more time, please?" I'm still not one hundred percent convinced that she was the one who hit the button.

Her face contorts and her head moves sideways across those critical inches—"Stephanie, that's the one I want."

Seeing a tear slide down Pam's cheek, I sit there with a lump in my throat—*that* was a purposeful movement, no doubt. Stephanie claps her hands in excitement and gets up to play the song. She didn't say, "Great job, Emmy!" or "Wow, I can't believe you used a switch for the first time!" In a way, it's as if she knew all along that her friend would get it. She never doubted.

Eventually the chorus of the song I've heard at least a hundred times this year struck up: "The way that you flip your hair gets me overwhelmed. But when you smile at the ground, it ain't hard to tell / You don't know, oh, oh, You don't know you're beaut——"

Abruptly the song stops. Stephanie's head jerks up with a look of shock. Pam's pointer-finger is on top of the space bar. "Sorry, Steph," she quickly says, "I just want to make sure that this is the song Emily really wanted."

Stephanie glares at Pam and then trains her eyes on me in a way that communicates, "Who is this lady who stopped my reward song?"

I smile and put up one finger to ask Stephanie to wait a second. I know Pam has purposely paused the song to get one more communication opportunity with Emily. Barb and Jan have stopped what they were doing and are slowly moving over to see what is about to happen.

Pam crouches before Emily and says, "Emily, you did so well! Was this the song you wanted to hear?" She again gently rubs the right side where the button sits inches from her head. This time, all of the class's eyes are trained on Emily.

"I hate this song," Devonte says in the background.

I laugh. "Sorry, Devonte, this is Emily's chance to pick."

We all stare at Emily. *C'mon, Emily, you can do it.* Ten seconds . . . fifteen seconds . . . twenty seconds pass, then suddenly that same grimace comes over her face. As her arms constrict toward her body, her head simultaneously moves more than the necessary two inches to hit the big red button—

"Stephanie, that's the one I want," the voice projects distinctly.

"Well, I'll be!" Jan crows.

"Can we play the song now?!" Stephanie implores with clear frustration in her voice.

Now it is Pam's turn to laugh. "Sorry, Stephanie. Yes, let's play it all the way through. I think it's safe to say that you and Emily share the same taste in music."

Stephanie hits the 'Play' button, and the tune picks up right where it left off. As the pop song plays on and verses and the chorus fill the room, none of the adults have dry eyes. When the final line, "That's what makes you beautiful" ends, Stephanie stands up and casually slides past all of us and returns to her desk as if nothing has happened. Stephanie will never fully understand how she opened up the world for her friend. Even if she did, she wouldn't look for praise for her idea. I'm pretty sure she would just say, "I want to help. Emmy is my friend."

CHAPTER NINE

OUR CLASSROOM GETS VERY good news this week, when I run into the school counselor assigned to our hall. She asks me if I remember Cory from last year who had to transfer to a different school due to poor attendance and constant trips to detention. I never really knew the details of Cory's troubles last year, and sometimes I honestly prefer not to know. I want to see those who come into this room only in light of what happens within our classroom. I know that's how our kids view the various adults and peer tutors who come into Room A113.

The one thing I know for certain about Cory from last year is that she loved to work with Justin, and she was his best friend at Twin Oaks. The counselor goes on to say that, with Cory's toxic biological father out of the picture because of the court stepping in, she has thrived in the stable foster home she was placed in, and is even attending weekly counseling sessions. Her new situation is not perfect, and there are scars from her childhood that I'm sure she will have to fight to recover from her whole life, but sometimes even the hope of being on the right road can be more transformative than any medicine.

At Cory's most recent meeting, the team decided after the growth she had shown that it would be best for her to be back at her hometown school, so she would return to Twin Oaks starting next week. I was so happy to hear all of this.

Sometimes it seems as if the stories are too heartbreaking and the obstacles too great for these young people to overcome. *What if I had been raised in Cory's home environment? How would I have turned out?* I wonder. Who knows why some people are able to persevere and make it when everything would point to them being whipped by life.

The counselor asks me if I would allow Cory to come back into my room as a peer tutor. I agree with a professional nod of my head and smile, but inside I am doing a fist-pump over this great news. The counselor stresses that Cory's behavior and classwork will be closely monitored to determine if she can continue to help in our class. I tell her I understand, but I let her know that Cory's return will be a win for our classroom, and that one student in particular will be absolutely thrilled about her reappearance.

I walk out the door pleased, not only about the news, but also that I didn't think once about my own issues, and my shirt was perfectly dry!

*   *   *   *

Waiting in the psychiatrist's office, I scan the environment. Outdated issues of *Sports Illustrated*, *Psychology Today*, and *Good Housekeeping* make large piles in the center table of the waiting room. A framed inspirational quote written in calligraphy hangs above the receptionist's desk:

Mental Illness is Not a Choice . . .
but Recovery is.

I pick up a sports magazine at random and read a preview for the 2010 NBA finals from two years ago. The sports pundit's prediction for the series is the Celtics going home to Boston as champions. How sweet that would have been. I know full well the grim results of that year's finals—Kobe and the Lakers will end up winning that series in seven.

I remember the first time I was in this office last year. I had been seeing Pastor Tim for about six months, when I finally admitted to myself that I needed additional help. In fact, it was Pastor Tim who asked me what my thoughts were on medication. I told him medication had always been a strange topic for me growing up. In all of my years of going to church camps, Sunday services, and Bible studies, we never really talked about mental health. Depression or anxiety issues were somewhat taboo topics, and when it was discussed it was mostly described as a symptom that needed healing through prayer or healthier living or whatnot. Now that I think about it, it was almost seen, even if not explicitly stated, as a lack of faith. The underlying message was, if you trusted in God, why would you have anxiety? Even though I was no longer going to church, having Tim give his pastoral blessing over giving medication a chance removed some sort of mental barrier for me.

*   *   *   *

I look around the office and observe the two other patients who have appointments with psychiatrists at the clinic. I wonder what their stories are? A woman in a navy pantsuit and white blouse is sporting a Bluetooth earpiece and reading a book on her Kindle. Next to her is a tall male, around my age, with dark gray slacks and a blue and white windowpane dress shirt. He is slowly sipping one of the office's free coffees and has a friendly-looking demeanor. I wouldn't be surprised at all if he were a teacher himself.

I continue to look down at my magazine, but am thinking about how we look like three well-adjusted, responsible adults, yet all of us are battling something so difficult that we have to come here in the middle of our workday for help. It is fascinating how the setting in which we meet someone can frame what we think about that person. If I saw these other two individuals at the T station or a Sox game, I wouldn't have any idea that they were struggling with something, but even without knowing the specifics, this waiting room has put all of us in the same boat.

Suddenly the click of the keys stops. The receptionist picks up the phone and looks up at me. "Michael, the doctor will see you now."

Today's appointment is pretty straightforward until the trajectory-changing moment at the end. The doctor is leaving the room, but then pauses at the door and looks back at me, as if remembering one last detail. "Have you ever tried Cognitive Behavior Therapy? It sounds like that might be a good fit for what you are describing. It has lots of research on its effectiveness, especially when paired with the right medication plan. The receptionist up front can refer you to a psychologist in our network who could provide that type of support."

Without even waiting for an answer from me, he leaves to see the next patient in his packed schedule. Even though it probably felt like a throwaway comment to him, that idea has opened up a whole new option for me, and a seed of possible help has been planted in my mind. Like our classroom peer tutor, Cory, I guess getting on a different road can give you a feeling of hope, and sometimes that feeling can make all the difference in the world.

CHAPTER TEN

I COME INTO SCHOOL earlier that Wednesday and sit down in my hand-me-down office chair with the slightly torn right armrest. I think about all the people who have passed through this classroom before me.

When I first entered this room nearly two years ago before the start of the school year, I found decades of accumulated materials. Pieces of schoolwork and visual schedules from years past were folded inside file cabinets. Teachers' last names from prior years marked the inside jackets of books bought for one set of kids, but left for future students. There were old VHS tapes, toys, and games with faded covers revealing the history of this room like the growth rings of a tree. I remember walking in that first day and starting to take inventory. Halfway through I realized that it was a huge waste of time.

As the year went on, the items started to get organized by Jan, Barbara, and me in a way that made sense to us. Schoolwork done by students who had moved on years ago was recycled, and materials that were of use to us found homes in logical spaces. Within three months the classroom was transformed from a place where I was a guest to a place that felt like home to the kids and us. I look around the walls and see student art from the last unit on Boston's history. I notice a line Barbara made with wide, red ribbon symbolizing the Freedom Trail of Boston. This actual trail has a red line made of brick and paint that runs through the city and links Boston's many historical sites such as the site of the Boston Massacre, Paul Revere's home, and the Old North Church, and ends with the monument at Bunker Hill.

I love looking at the wall because of the story it tells, both in terms of America's history as well as the story of our students. You can see the students' styles and preferences stamped on each piece of work.

Stephanie loves to paint, so we got a wooden model ship to represent the USS Constitution. She and a peer tutor from Mrs. Liu's class worked together, carefully painting the ship in way that was befitting of "Old Ironsides," a ship that was never defeated in battle.

Justin enjoys taking pictures, so when we took our class trip to see the actual sites of the trail, he took an impressively framed photo of the Boston Latin School, the first public school of the United States. In his picture you can see Jan and Stevie giving a big thumbs-up next to the statue of one of the school's most famous dropouts, Benjamin Franklin.

Devonte has created an art piece to represent the famous "one if by land, two if by sea" lanterns that were hung in the Old North Church. Two shoebox bottoms have been painted black, and battery-powered candles, leftover from last Halloween, have been suspended inside. His two lanterns hang from the ceiling and proudly shine a light on our students' work.

The wall may not display a two-page expository essay like those in the other Twin Oaks classrooms, but it shows that our students understand the material in their own ways. Devonte can recite facts from the wall, and Molly will point to a Christmas ornament horse when asked what Paul Revere rode that historic night. It is our job as teachers to figure out how to help students express their knowledge in a way that makes sense to them. That problem-solving aspect of Special Education is something I will always love about this job.

*   *   *   *

I have my first appointment with Dr. Givens, the psychologist I was referred to earlier. Unfortunately, the only time slot available is right in the middle of my workday. I hate having to call in for a half-day substitute, but I figure it was worth it to meet this doctor.

She begins by getting to know my story, then she asks me some rather unexpected questions. "So, Michael," she says, "I was wondering if you could answer 'yes' or 'no' to the following questions."

I always get nervous with giving only 'yes' or 'no' responses. You are at the mercy of only two choices—no elaborating, no explaining. An image of Emily's *Big Mac* button appears in my mind, but the thought is quickly interrupted as the first round of questions begins.

"Do you ever fear you might harm someone, for example, with a kitchen knife or a baseball bat?" I shake my head "no," but I think she sees the alarm on my face, because she follows up with, "I know a lot of these questions may seem intense or embarrassing, but they are needed in order to get a fuller picture of you." Dr. Givens continues, "Do you see violent or horrific images in your mind—ones that cause you distress?" I tell her that I don't think so, but I am still somewhat confused by the line of questioning:

"Do you have a fear of blurting out obscenities?"

"Do you fear you will steal something?"

"Do you have concern with dirt or germs?"

Her questions are all met with "no" responses from me.

Finally, Dr. Givens asks a new set of questions:

"Do you have an inordinate amount of fear of what others are thinking about you?"

"Do you fear that actions will be interpreted as unwanted advances?"

"Do you have excessive concerns about being morally right or wrong?"

They are unnerving in their accuracy of describing the fears and insecurities I have been trying to suppress for years. I hesitantly say "yes" to all of them as my hands fidget in my lap. Dr. Givens keeps going. Some responses are a strong "no," and others are, "Yeah, I guess so."

After going through the questionnaire, I experience a feeling of shame. I look at Dr. Givens as she controls my fate now. *Would she say that I have mental issues that are going to lead to serious trouble? That these thoughts are very frightening and say a lot of negative things about the real me? That I'm incurable and unfit to work with kids?* I feel a suffocating tightness in my chest as I wait for the verdict to be handed down by a person whom I had only met one hour prior. What would the sum of my responses end up saying about me?

Dr. Givens breaks the tension, though, with a sudden smile. Just when I think she will reveal the results of my "test," she follows up with, "Okay, Michael, I'm going to be asking you another set of questions. I know these questions can be hard, but you are doing great. Are you ready?"

I start to sweat, look down, and mumble, "Sorry, the sweating is what happens when I feel anxious. It's not you. Do you have a napkin or Kleenex I could use?"

Dr. Givens gets me a tissue and says it was honestly hardly noticeable. After a thirty-second break, we are back to Round Two.

After the final question is asked, she clicks her pen shut. "So I guess you are wondering why I asked you all of these unusual questions?"

I actually figured it out around midway through the second set of questions, when she asked about hand-washing, checking and re-checking doors, and rearranging objects. So I offer, "You think I might have OCD?"

"So, maybe this won't come as much of a surprise to you as I thought, but yes, I believe that is a possibility."

I am still taken aback. I have always thought of Obsessive Compulsive Disorder as what the doctor character Michael J. Fox had on the show *Scrubs*. He couldn't stop washing his hands, no matter how hard he tried. Then there was a guy on the second floor of my dorm building who would check and recheck if he had locked his door five to six times before slowly joining the rest of us to head to the cafeteria, then after a few steps he would sprint back with an embarrassed look for one final check. I didn't have any of those tendencies. How could Dr. Givens suggest I had OCD?

I finally decide that I need to speak up. "I guess I'm just not sure I see it the same way. Couldn't I be just an overly-anxious person who gets super-nervous about things like eye contact. Doesn't that sound more like social anxiety than OCD?"

"That's true, and I'm not discounting social anxiety as part of the equation," she says in a non-dismissive way. "The two, however, can be closely linked. I read an article the other day that showed how people with a primary diagnosis of OCD are more at risk to be impacted by a Social Anxiety Disorder as well. Let's explore that more during our next session."

She pauses briefly to let me digest the information, then concludes, "I want you to think past the label of OCD and how it is portrayed in movies. I think the core problem isn't that you are fixated on your eye contact or how you ruminate on how others are perceiving your interaction. It's that you feel the need to do your rituals and routines to help alleviate the anxiety you feel—almost like trying to extinguish a fire by fanning it down. Your intentions are good, but your actions are reinforcing the compulsions and helping fuel the very thing you are trying to eliminate. If you decide that you would like to work together, we will learn to sit through your anxiety and accept the feelings as they come, as opposed to combating them with compulsive routines."

Although thinking of myself as OCD is disconcerting, Dr. Givens' tentative diagnosis makes some sense, which gives me a strange sense of relief. The lens through which I view myself has shifted quite a bit in one ninety-minute intake session.

CHAPTER ELEVEN

THIS MORNING STEVIE FOLLOWS his recent practice of dropping off his backpack and making a beeline straight to the phone atop the four-drawer file cabinet beside our kitchen area. Stevie is short in stature, so he is just tall enough to reach the telephone, but can't quite see the numbers. He will rush in, do a full-arm stretch to grab the phone, and then start having an imaginary conversation with someone from his family. Yesterday he said, "Hi Gramma... yes, okay... I will, Gramma... Okay, bye, Gramma... bye." Then he hung up the phone and went about his morning routine.

Barb isn't too big of a fan of students playing with teacher materials, and she is probably in the right with this one. However, I get a feeling that this is worth exploring, so I say, "Let's see if we can use the phone to work on Stevie's language." I was thinking he loves to talk but has a limited range of topics. I wonder if we could use this opportunity to increase his topic base and improve his give-and-take in conversations as well.

Barb gives me "the look"—not mean in any way, but it was clear she was still not sold on the idea of using our phone as a teaching tool. I laugh, "You are probably right, Barb. If this blows up in my face and other teachers start getting mysterious phone calls from Stevie asking for 'Gramma,' then I will take the blame."

Barb finally cracks a wry grin and says it's a deal. I catch Stevie's eye, pick up my phone, and start off the play scenario with, "Hello, is Stevie there?"

Stevie looks surprised at first, but then he smiles and looks down at the ground, as if we are having a real conversation, not from five feet away but miles apart. He gives his classic greeting, "Hiiiii Mr. Sniiiifff!"

"Hey, what's up, Stevie? Good talking to you over the phone. I just wanted to call and see what you brought for lunch today."

"Chocolate surprise!" he says cheerfully. I assume that this is some sort of cake, so I follow his lead and tell him how great that sounds. I ask if there's anything else. Stevie pauses, then gives more thought than usual to one of my questions: "Chiiips and sandwich."

I am blown away. This is one of the rare times Stevie has ever deviated from his favorite phrases and responded to a topic I've initiated. I smile, knowing this is why I love this job.

"What kind of sandwich?" I ask Stevie, hoping we can somehow keep this conversation going.

"Ham... yuuukkk!" Stevie says with a strong emphasis on the "k."

Well, I guess I learned a couple of new things about Stevie this morning—talking on the phone can draw more language out of him, and he has no love for his mom's ham sandwiches. I look over to him as we end the conversation. "Okay, well, maybe we can find you a little something extra in the cafeteria. Sound good? I've got to go to class now. It was really nice talking to you, Stevie. Have a good morning."

"Okay, bye... bye, Mr. Sniiiiff."

*   *   *   *

On Cory's first day back, two weeks ago, she came in, and Justin stopped looking at the lights and paused his self-stimming with his fingers. He did a small little hop and laugh in his seat, rocking back and forth with happy recognition. Cory returned his positive gestures with a wide smile. I was actually somewhat amazed that Justin could see that this was his old friend. Gone was her unkempt long black hair and Goth-inspired attire. Instead, her natural-brown hair was pulled back into a ponytail, and she wore a bright orange and blue plaid shirt—the upbeat colors matching the mood of the room. The smile was the same, but she had a different aura about her. It was as if the dark cloud enveloping her last school year had lifted.

Cory sits with Justin, as has been her routine since reintegrating into our class. I get the room's attention with chimes that signal a transition, and then tell them we will be doing something new for math today. At the front of the room I have set up a small class store made up of old sports posters, Disney key chains, and nineties Beanie Babies, all found in the back closet area. Each item had a sticky-note price tag with a dollar and change amount. We would be working on paying for the items with "the next dollar" strategy.

Devonte is first to go, and he heads straight to the old Red Sox Nomar Garciaparra poster for $2.99—no surprise there. When setting up the class store before the kids came in from recess, I had stopped and stared at the old Red Sox legend's poster, and, as is so often the case with me and baseball, memories from old times past came flooding back.

*   *   *   *

When you live in a city like Portland, Oregon, which doesn't have a baseball franchise, you sometimes choose your team for the most arbitrary of reasons. For me, it was opening a Topps baseball card pack on my twelfth birthday and finding a Nomar Garciaparra card on top of the deck. I don't know what it was about that card in particular that made it my instant favorite. Maybe it was his cool, confident expression, juxtaposed with the violent twist of his body, as he made square contact with the ball. Or maybe it was the way the background of the card reflected the light, signifying that this was a rare card that probably had extra value.

Whatever the reason, that day I chose Nomar as my favorite player, which in turn made the Red Sox my new favorite team. Then, I guess, if you want to extrapolate it an embarrassing step further, almost six years later, when I began to look at colleges, Boston schools were the only ones at the top of my wish list. I don't know what that says about me and my priorities, but I have Nomar and the rest of the late-nineties Red Sox team to thank for making a random kid from Portland a Boston sports fan and introducing me to this great city.

There was a time when Nomar was the hope of Red Sox baseball. He had that something special, something that made you think that only talent like his could overcome any eighty-year-old curse that you were always reminded about on Sports Center. During that 1998 season when I got his card, I woke up every morning, and the first thing I did was go downstairs to check box scores in *The Oregonian* to read how my favorite team and favorite player did the previous day. If he had a particularly great game, I'd sometimes even cut out the box score to save for later.

Then what happened to their old team captain in 2004? Before the season started, Nomar suffered an Achilles' heel injury that kept him off the opening day lineup, and slowed him down after his return. Ultimately the team decided to trade Nomar halfway through the season to an even more cursed franchise, the Chicago Cubs. The story gets worse, or better, depending on your view. That year the Red Sox break 86 years of pain and torment in the most improbable fashion, coming back from 0-3 to the New York Yankees in the playoffs, and then go on to beat the Cardinals to win the World Series. Where was Nomar during that time? Kind of like Moses in the wilderness, he never made it into the Promised Land with the group he once led. Who knows why things work out the way they do? Bad luck? Not meant to be? Either way, kind of makes you wonder if there are some "Achilles' heels" that get too injured to ever overcome.

*   *   *   *

Devonte does an excellent job demonstrating the dollar-up math skill and talking through his purchase. "Poster is two dollars and ninety-nine cents," he starts in his higher voice. "The next number after two is three." His voice suddenly drops an octave lower as he finishes the problem: "I will give three dollars."

"Awesome job, Devonte! Here you go, one Nomar poster for you!" I hand off the poster and give him a quick high-five. I am super-proud and impressed that Devonte has this skill down. It's a functional skill that will serve him well in the future.

Devonte looks pleased and smiles at the poster, which was probably made right around the time he was born. I turn my attention back to the class and keep the lesson moving forward. "All right, let's keep the positive momentum going—who's next, guys? Stephanie, I see a Backstreet Boys poster that I think might have your name on it." Stephanie gives an over-exaggerated eye roll. I guess her faithfulness to her boy band is stronger than I thought. I laugh, "Okay, we will come back to you, Steph. How about you, Justin? See anything here you'd like to purchase?" I look over at Cory, who reads my cue, and with a nurturing voice urges Justin to stand up.

With fake money in hand Justin shuffles toward the front of the classroom. As he approaches the store, he suddenly stops. His face grimaces, as if he has just bitten into a wad of aluminum foil. He makes a low rumbling sound from deep in his chest, which quickly progresses to an ear-piercing scream. Justin flings his stack of fake bills up in the air. With one hand tightly clenching his ear he heads straight toward Stevie with his other hand in a closed fist raised above his head. It all happens so quickly that I don't have time to react. With the last bills still falling around us, Justin takes his clenched fist and hammers straight down on Stevie's unsuspecting face. Cory lets out a small scream. Stevie cradles his face and starts to cry, his feet kicking back and forth from the pain. Barb rushes over and positions herself between Stevie and Justin. I run up to Justin and steer him by the shoulders to the side of the classroom. Justin is already moaning, "Oowwww! Owwwww!" He looks over at me, then grabs his wrist and pulls back, ready to take out all of what he is feeling, this time on his own nose. I am ready, and snatch his right hand and wrestle it down. I react instinctively, and use what was practiced earlier this year during my restraint training. Even though Justin is relatively skinny for a middle schooler, his adrenaline is giving him extra strength. This makes it difficult to get him in a safe position, but eventually I take hold of his other wrist, and cross his two arms in front of his body, locking them under his armpits. His arms held in this "W" shape keep him from striking again. He is struggling and screeching loudly—this is definitely not comfortable for him or me.

While I am focused on Justin, Jan is already herding the kids out the door to the playground. I glance up and see Barb tending to Stevie, who looks more shocked than seriously hurt at this point. Barb asks Cory if she wouldn't mind walking Stevie to the nurse's office, as she plans to help me with Justin. Cory puts her arm around Stevie's shoulder, but looks noticeably shaken herself. Barb then heads to the phone to call the office. Every time I think Justin is about to calm down, a jolt of adrenaline courses through his body, and I can feel his muscles tighten and strengthen as he tries to break free from my grasp. This forces me to hold on all the tighter. I hate this—I pray that I am not hurting him.

We are currently on the ground, him in a sitting position, arms still set in a W, and me positioned behind him, holding his arms as best I can. I keep my head to one side in case he tries to break free with a head-butt, but thankfully it never comes to that. "Please, Justin, breathe, buddy. You can do it."

Mr. Ballamy enters the room, looking wide-eyed at the scene playing out in front of him. "You guys okay? What do you need me to do?" he asks in his coach's voice.

"I don't think we are okay yet, Mr. Ballamy. I think Justin will begin to calm down pretty soon." Justin's face muscles tighten and contract, tighten and contract. I qualify my statement slightly, "But I'm not sure how long this will last."

I hear Mr. Ballamy change his tone of voice trying to calm Justin down. What a heartbreaking thing. Something so out of everyone's control, and now Stevie pays the price too. What is happening? Why does it feel like we are going in the wrong direction with Justin? I finally start to feel the tension slowly beginning to leave his body, and thankfully I can begin to release my hold on him.

CHAPTER TWELVE

I CALL STEVIE'S MOM, Mrs. Bell, at lunch to fill her in on today's events. The conversation goes as well as I could hope. I don't use Justin's name, but I do explain to her the events that led up to the quarter-sized goose-egg above Stevie's left eye. Mrs. Bell asks if her son provoked the other student. I tell her he didn't, and Stevie was just in the wrong place at the wrong time. I say this student has never acted aggressively toward peers before, so I'm hopeful that this was a one-time event. In my mind, I know we'll be meeting with the behaviorist tomorrow to review Justin's behavior plan and to figure out better ways to support him and keep Stevie and all the other kids safe.

Mrs. Bell is probably more gracious than I would be if my child were hit by another student. I think it must be a hard thing for a mother of a child with special needs to process. Although her own experiences with Stevie have made her more empathetic toward unexpected behaviors, her utmost concern will always be for her son and his safety. She is understanding, yet makes it clear that if another incident like this occurs she will follow up with Special Education administration.

I worry about Justin. Is a future injury to himself or someone else inevitable? Is he even safe to ride the bus home anymore? These are not the scenarios you envision when you first dream of going into Special Education.

*   *   *   *

I step into the waiting room and greet the receptionist. It's a different feeling than walking into the familiarity of Pastor Tim's office. Now I feel a mixture of nervousness and hope regarding this new perspective Dr. Givens is offering me.

As I sit down, Dr. Givens asks me about my week, and I start to feel that unwanted rush of heat that happens when I'm put on the spot and asked to talk about myself. While we carry on with our small talk, my mind begins to race as I see Dr. Givens glance away. *What did that glance mean?* I think. *Was I making even this new doctor uncomfortable with my eye contact? Does she think I'm trying to make advances toward her even though she looks twice my age?* I know these concerns aren't reasonable, but they still feel real, and make me sweat all the more.

Unwelcome thoughts continue to tumble around my mind, I close my eyes a second longer to keep from making prolonged eye contact with the doctor. I am cognizant of the duration of each blink, like a metronome counting the beats—eyes open, 1, 2, 3, 4, and shut, 1, 2.

This keeps going, as I'm half-focused on the timing of my eye contact and also trying to concentrate on Dr. Givens' plan for today's session. After a second, Dr. Givens stops and asks kindly, "Michael, is there something wrong with your eyes? You seem to be blinking differently than you normally do."

I feel the combination of embarrassment, stupidity, and shame. "No, no, I'm fine—I mean, yes, you are right," I respond. "I was thinking about eye contact while you were talking, and I guess I thought holding my blink longer might help make things more comfortable for you."

Dr. Givens gives me an understanding, judgment-free smile. "Michael, this is actually a perfect example of a compulsive behavior. For you, the obsessive thoughts you have are pretty easy to identify. For instance, just now you were thinking about eye contact and how it was making me feel—which, for the record, fell completely within the normal range." This is the affirmation I longed to hear, but was too afraid to ask. Dr. Givens continues, "Were there any other thoughts that you were fixated on?"

I tell her about what was making me feel uneasy, starting with the eye contact, and then fearing that it appeared I was making advances toward her. "It really freaks me out, Dr. Givens. I don't like these thoughts, and I know deep down they are untrue. But if they are not true, why can't my mind dismiss them? Maybe I was blinking longer because subconsciously I was thinking that a moment of less eye contact was somehow less threatening. I can't explain it. It sounds so stupid when I say it out loud."

"First off, it's not stupid," she says. "Second, the fact that a thought is unwanted tells me how unlikely these fears are ever to play out."

Her reassurances and insight help bring a level of comfort into the conversation, so I share, "The harder I try not to think about an uncomfortable thought, whether it is eye-contact, the fear that women think I'm coming on to them, or constantly monitoring my sweating, the louder these thoughts show up next time. I do lots of self-talk, positive affirmations, mantras I've learned, but those only seem to help so much. I'm really tired . . . mentally, emotionally, and even physically from when my body goes into an all-out sweat mode. I know something has to change, but there is no solution that I can see."

For a moment toward the end I almost forgot I was talking to Dr. Givens. Rarely do I speak such personal thoughts out loud.

"I'm glad that we are working together, Michael," she reassures me. "It does sound burdensome to wrestle with all those thoughts and emotions all day long. My job is to help you separate the emotions from the unwanted thoughts, and to see them for what they are—just thoughts. Right now you interpret your sweating, your eye contact, and negative thoughts as actual threats—but they are not! They are random and inexplicable, and we will learn to identify, acknowledge, and release those thoughts without giving them more weight than they deserve."

Dr. Givens glances over at the clock, and my eyes follow her gaze. About fifteen minutes are left in our session. As she continues, my mind is fully engaged in the conversation, no longer thinking about my own eye contact with her.

She taps the back of her pen on her yellow legal pad. "The long, extended blinking is an example of some of your compulsive behaviors that feed your anxiety. You had some thoughts that made you uncomfortable, so what did you do? You tried to 'fix it' with a prolonged blink. On the surface that may seem harmless, but that act worked as a compulsion that didn't actually make the situation better. It's the same with the self-talk or positive affirmations you mentioned earlier. Are those things truly giving you relief, or lessening the power of those thoughts?"

I agree that they aren't, at least not in the long run.

"Michael, some would even argue that avoidant behavior can be looked on as an act of compulsion, inadvertently reinforcing the obsession that the only way to not be exposed to anxiety-provoking situations is to avoid them all together."

As she expounds on her position, the murky and confusing 'C' in OCD starts to form into a picture that makes sense to me. My mind flashes back to sitting in the parking lot that first time, waiting to meet Pastor Tim, that day the church building came into sharper view as I shifted my eyes beyond the rain-covered windshield. For some reason, talking to Dr. Givens today feels similar. A new mental image has emerged as my focus has changed.

$$* \qquad * \qquad * \qquad *$$

On my next visit to Dr. Givens I am a little more relaxed and start making observations about her waiting room. It's much simpler than that of the psychiatrist whom I had seen previously. This time I see no framed inspirational quotes or peaceful fountain bubbling over a miniature rock garden, just some simple beachscape prints lining the light gray walls.

What remains constant between both offices, though, is the coffee table with stacks of magazines. As I leaf through the pile, one bold title catches my eye: "Where are They Now? 20 Years Later: Olympic Edition." I recognize the two athletes on the cover instantly: Dan O'Brien and Dave Johnson from Reebok's famous—or maybe infamous—Dan & Dave ad campaign. I was only six years old when the Dan & Dave commercials were run to hype the competition between these two decathletes prior to the 1992 Barcelona Olympics.

The article details the story of the two previously unknown Olympic hopefuls who became world-famous overnight with the "Who is the World's Greatest Athlete?" ads that initially ran during the Super Bowl. The story goes on to talk about how Reebok's twenty-five-million-dollar marketing plan was so successful that industry giants like Nike were legitimately worried about competition from this burgeoning shoe company.

Being a sports nerd, I knew all about the anticipation that swept over the country for this decathlon showdown at the Olympics. The funny commercials fueled excitement over whether Dan or Dave would be crowned the World's Greatest Athlete.

I also knew the horrible climax of their shared story when, during the preliminary trials, Dan O'Brien received zero points in the pole vault event, and failed to even qualify for the Olympics. In three missed attempts to clear the bar, he destroyed his dreams, as well as somewhat derailed Reebok's advertisement plan. As I wait and read, I remember the redeeming aspects of the story—Dave persevered through a stress fracture in his foot to win bronze in those Olympic games, and Dan eventually won gold four years later in the Atlanta Olympics.

One part of this story, however, is new and stands out to me. Apparently, after Dan failed to qualify in 1992, he started to get panic-attack-like symptoms before track events and even contemplated quitting the sport. Instead of ending his career, though, he chose to see a sports psychologist. After working together, the two of them did something Dan had avoided for three years: watching the three failed pole vault attempts on video. It was literally the first time Dan had laid eyes on the recorded testimony of his failed attempts, and in an instant all of his negative emotions and pain about them came rushing back. After having Dan relive the traumatic event, his psychologist rewound the tape, and they watched it again. In fact, they watched it over and over until seeing what Dan viewed as his biggest athletic failure did not have the same effect on him. I smile as I read how Dan O'Brien faced his demons and how those missed pole vault attempts and failure to qualify for the Olympics didn't ultimately define him.

I put the magazine away as the door between the doctors' offices and waiting room opens. Dr. Givens raises her hand with a casual greeting, and I follow her back to her office.

*   *   *   *

During today's session, Dr. Givens introduces a new Cognitive Behavioral Therapy concept that she says will be a helpful tool, given my social anxiety and OCD tendencies. She calls it Exposure and Response Prevention Therapy, and the idea is to face your fearful situations and triggers and learn to ride out the wave of anxiety until the feeling passes. To help explain, she draws a graph in the shape of a bell curve. The end points are labeled "Calm State." Along the left, ascending side of the hill, she writes "Anxiety Increasing." The pinnacle she labels "Panic Peak," and along the right, downward slope she writes "Riding it Down."

The image of the graph reminds me of a ride like Splash Mountain—the nervous anticipation as you chug up the hill, the pause at the top when your heart rate doubles, the gravitational free-fall, and finally the return to terra firma. Dr.

Givens touches her pen to the start of the graph and begins to trace along the upward arc as she talks.

"So, to make this relevant to what you experience—say, for example, you are worried that your co-worker is disturbed by your eye contact. Instead of doing what you usually do—escaping the situation, thinking of reaffirming mantras, or using prolonged blinks, when you're here"—she points to the apex—"we will learn more productive actions, such as deep breathing or learning to accept what is happening around you. I want to work with you on sitting through your most anxious moments, knowing that your anxiety levels will rise but will also always eventually come back down."

She finishes tracing along the downward slope and holds down her pen on "Calm State." "Remember, uncomfortable thoughts and automatic physical reactions will occur, and there is very little we can do about that. How we respond to those thoughts, though, will not only impact our current experience, but also reinforce what is likely to happen during future events as well."

Her suggestion not to rely on my normal strategies is puzzling and disconcerting. *You mean I've been following the wrong advice all this time?* My face must clearly reflect my confusion—I always have had a terrible poker face—because Dr. Givens asks me what is causing my distress. I admit that I don't understand how escaping an anxiety-producing situation or dwelling on positive phrases can be bad.

She does not seem offended by my questioning her professional opinion, but calmly states, "I agree, for most people that is a fine and effective strategy for dealing with anxiety. However, what I'm proposing is that the root of your problem, the OCD component, may be very different than what is the cause of other people's anxieties. Because of that difference, we need to individualize a plan that works to help you, not reinforce the very behaviors and rituals we are trying to extinguish."

What Dr. Givens says makes sense. The word *individualize* reminds me of my own students. I think of Devonte and Molly, both of whom are on the autism spectrum, but who require very different types of support to help them be successful. Another connection is the bell curve she draws. It is very similar to a diagram taught to us during a behavior management course in graduate school for understanding and working with a student who is in crisis mode. The memory of Justin and what happened the other day with Stevie comes to mind—we tried to prevent the rise of emotion and frustration, but when that point of no return came, we could do nothing but ride it out and keep everyone safe until the emotional peak hit and he eventually was able to return to a calm state again.

I like Dr. Givens. She has already become another steadying presence in my life. I no longer view her as the person who gained access to my private thoughts too quickly through a yes/no questionnaire during our first session. We set up our next appointment, and she previews it by sharing that we will be practicing Exposure and Response Prevention Therapy, with the goal of continuing to ratchet up the intensity of each exposure during subsequent weeks.

Dr. Givens doesn't sugarcoat it. "It will be difficult, Michael. But that is the point—we will start off with small exposures such as looking at pictures of people's eyes or imagining face-to-face eye contact. During the following weeks, if you are ready, we will start to have one-on-one conversations with some of my colleagues, who will help us out. You will work on making eye contact and being okay with the sweat that I'm hoping we can elicit during your exposures. Finally, we will bring the most challenging types of scenarios to you—having the room intentionally hot on purpose and having others comment on your sweat or eye contact making them feel uncomfortable."

My chest tightens just imagining these scenarios. I tell her, though, that I'm ready to do whatever it takes, if it will help me. Unexpectedly, the images of Dan O'Brien re-watching his failed pole vault attempt again and again in his sports psychologist's office runs through my mind.

After Dr. Givens and I agree to the game plan, there is a pause in our conversation. She finally breaks the silence with, "I was thinking, too, like your students you talked about last session, you feel pride when they do the best they can with the obstacles they face. Don't forget to be proud of yourself every now and then for doing the best you can with the obstacles you face—both in here with our upcoming exposure sessions and also out there in the real world."

I tell Dr. Givens I really appreciate what she said. Walking out the building to my car, I feel a happiness I hadn't felt in a while. I'm not entirely sure why—maybe it was just knowing how fortunate I was to have people who cared, like Pastor Tim and Dr. Givens, walking alongside me. As I close the door to my car, I say, "Thank you," quietly under my breath. I'm not exactly sure who this comment is intended for, but it's probably the closest thing to a prayer I've uttered in the last four years.

CHAPTER THIRTEEN

EVERY COUPLE OF MONTHS I try to plan a community outing of some sort for my students. We used to call them "field trips," but "community-based instruction" has a higher likelihood of funding approval.

The zoo trip is an annual tradition for this program. It is a perfect Thursday in May on the east coast. We haven't had snowfall in multiple weeks, so no big piles of dirty, brown snow line the roadways. Instead, it is a sunny, clear day with temperatures approaching seventy degrees. After any New England winter, even a mild one like the one we just experienced, having weather like this so early in the year perks up the mood of even the most crusty Bostonian.

For the community outing we will have all of our students: Justin, Stevie, Molly, Emily, Stephanie, and Devonte. We also usually invite two or three peer tutors from Ms. Liu's class to join us. They absolutely love the field trips! Not only do they get to hang out with their friends from our class, but what middle-school student wouldn't want to miss school for four hours to go to the zoo? I was a little jittery after last week's episode with Justin, but I remembered that there was no real precursor to the behavior that we had found, and he was honestly just as likely to have a moment at school as at a public facility. So I take a deep breath and hope for the best.

These trips used to give me nervous fits. Weeks in advance I would plan, check and recheck all of the details of the outing. While still diligent in preparing, I am now more relaxed about the process. Jan, Barbara, and I go through our pre-field trip routine, and we are ready to roll. Nurse Nancy unfortunately is unable to go, but Emily's mom gave the okay for a substitute nurse to go with us.

"Jan, how's Stevie doing? Can you encourage him to go to the bathroom one more time?"

"Barbara, how is the travel bag? Wipes? Extra changes of clothes? Contact info cards?"

I see the familiar substitute nurse, Linda. I greet her and pass along Emily's healthcare plan. "The supplies are all there," I tell her. "Can you just check to make sure that the EpiPen is in her bag?"

The substitute nurse looks in the back pocket of the wheelchair and gives me a thumbs-up.

"I think that's it," I say to the teachers, Linda, and the peer tutors. "Let's run final bathroom checks and then head to the bus."

We are ready in record time, and the kids have a little extra pep in their step, which makes sense. Who doesn't love the zoo?

*   *   *   *

The rhetorical question of "Who doesn't love the zoo?" I now realize is a little premature. Molly is not a fan of the zoo. I don't know if it is the change in her routine, or just the place itself, but she is beginning to shut down. When this happens, she ends up squatting and doing a nervous tick with her hand, where she takes both pointer fingers, curls them up, and digs the nails under her thumbnails. You can always tell when she is especially stressed, because her thumbs are extremely red or even start to bleed. Unfortunately, thirty minutes after passing through the gate, she is already approaching the bleeding level. After each stop, when our group is ready to move on, there is always a spirited test of wills between Molly and Barbara, who is assigned to stay with her.

We are getting ready to leave the underground Polar Bear exhibit, an area that captivated Justin as much as any community outing experience. Whenever the bear yawns, slides into the water or does graceful barrel rolls, Justin lets out a loud laugh and claps his hands in appreciation. Stephanie is helping to push Emily and loves to point out all of her favorite parts of the zoo to her friend.

I can tell Barb is getting pretty frustrated with Molly, so I tell her to go ahead with the others and see the giraffes while I walk with Molly and see if I can get her going a little faster. Molly is in her crouched position, slightly moaning, and still picking hard at the insides of her thumbs.

"It's all right, Molly," I say as reassuringly as possible, "you look ready to leave this place. Should we head outside and meet up with the rest of the class now?"

"No!" she says in her anxious, high-pitched voice, so we continue to sit there. I study Molly while we wait. One thing that I'm learning is that less language is often better with our crew. My natural instinct would be to strike up a conversation and try to distract her from whatever is bothering her—talk about Molly's favorite animals or something she likes at home. I know from experience, though, when her anxiety is this elevated, the more words I use, the more she retreats into her inner world. Even positive words can overload her and cause her to shut down.

I remember reading a passage from the book *The Curious Incident of the Dog in the Nighttime* about a boy with autism, in which the author, Mark Haddon, described language overload as being like a bread machine that cuts bread into slices and then readies itself for the next loaf. However, the bread machine can sometimes get logjammed, and all of a sudden bread is not getting sliced anymore, but more loaves keep coming. I know it's dangerous to generalize one person's experience with autism to anyone else's; even with similar characteristics, autism is a broad spectrum that manifests itself in many different ways. Looking at Molly, though, I think the bread-cutting analogy is pretty accurate. She needs time to gather her thoughts and get everything organized in her own mind before she is ready to move on. She doesn't need more questions or even more well-meaning words of encouragement from me.

After several minutes of silence, I ask Molly if she is ready to go.

"Yes!" she says in a slightly high-pitched voice, letting me know she is still anxious but regulated enough to meet up with the rest of the class. The two of us walk through the rest of the cave, along the path, and toward the back end of the giraffe enclosure. I expect to see all of our class waiting outside. No one is there. *Interesting*, I think.

Suddenly I hear a familiar sound from my phone: **Beeep** I start to reach for my device when I hear another **Beeep**, and another—**Beeep** **Beeep** **Beeep** The missed text messages flash in rapid-fire on my phone screen. I must have been in an out-of-service area down below with Molly. My chest tightens and my forehead begins to sweat as I look at my messages:

Message 1, 10:48 Emily having allergic reaction by giraffes! Linda used EpiPen. Come asap!

Message 2, 10:53 Your phones still going straight to VM! Come quick please!

Message 3, 10:55 Need you now Michael! Emily still not looking good after EpiPen. Calling 911

Message 4, 10:59 Sent peer tutor she didn't see you. Where are you?!!

There is a trick available in case of emergencies that works in getting Molly to move when really needed. She loves having her purse with her on these community trips, and she becomes very possessive of it. It causes a scene to take her purse from her, because she will scream and cry and chase after it. But when you need her to go, this always works. I grab Molly's purse and say, "C'mon, Molly, we gotta go!"

Molly, caught off-guard, lets out a blood-curdling scream and wails as we race through the zoo. All eyes are on us, but it doesn't matter. We need to get to Emily, who is probably at the front of the zoo by now. I spur Molly forward, enticing her with the purse. She lopes after me with her wide-gaited run. We weave through people and finally get to the entrance. My heart is thumping and my face is pouring sweat as we see the ambulance at the front gate.

Emily has already been taken out of her chair and is being strapped to a gurney. Her skin is an ashy blue, and her eyes are open but rolled back. I look at my watch—it reads 11:12. The first text was sent at 10:48. One EMT gives her an oxygen mask while another checks her vitals. My last image of Emily is with her eyes looking upward, her mouth contorted. Then my view is obstructed as the ambulance doors are slammed shut.

Everything feels like a dream, but I know what I have to do, and I pull out my phone. The screen is still on the chain of text messages documenting the minutes of horror I had no idea were occurring less than three hundred yards away outside the giraffe house. I close my eyes, pull out the emergency contact sheet from the backpack, and dial the ten-digit number.

"Hello, Mr. Smith," I hear warmly from the other end of the phone, "anything wrong?"

I swallow and begin, "Hi, Ms. Thompkins." I feel her side go quiet as she senses the tone of my voice. "It's Emily . . ."

CHAPTER FOURTEEN

ONCE AGAIN I FIND myself in a waiting room, but this time it is not for me. How I wish to God it was for me—that I were the one in that emergency room who experienced loss of oxygen from another allergic reaction! Although they are divorced, Emily's dad, John Thompkins, is sitting next to Ms. Thompkins, consoling her with one arm draped over her sagging shoulders.

I sit alone at the other side of the room to give the family space. I'm trying to process the awful events of the morning, but the severity and shock of it all makes it hard to focus on any one thought for too long. *How did this happen? Why didn't the EpiPen take care of everything? Why didn't the nurse call 911 immediately? I just don't understand . . .*

I overhear Ms. Thompkins and Mr. Thompkins talking to the doctor who has just entered the room, "Yes, that is me. How is she? She's okay, right? She didn't lose anymore functioning, right?"

The doctor takes a big big breath, then closes his eyes and bows his head. "I'm sorry—we did everything we could."

The loud wail from Rachael Thompkins fills the waiting room.

*   *   *   *

I sit in my car in the hospital parking lot, staring out the window for a moment, then mindlessly start it up. The empty darkness of the starless night sky seems fitting of today's events. I realize I am alone for the first time since the start of this day. I am unable to drive off, so I turn off the engine and weep.

*   *   *   *

It is a warm spring day. The number of floor fans spread out across the room spinning on 'high' signals that summer is not too far away. It is the first open-casket wake I have ever attended. My thoughts about Emily and her family are superseding my typical racing thoughts and irrational fears. I have been weighed down with the knowledge that one family could experience two deaths for the same daughter. The first death was when their daughter lost the ability to function as she once had. The second was when the rest of their Em was completely taken from them.

As healing was beginning and a new hopeful chapter of Emily's life was being written, the book is suddenly slammed shut. She was taken from her original group of middle school friends a couple of years back, with whom I pictured her gossiping and laughing outside her locker as the transition bell rang. Now she has been taken from her new friends, like Stephanie and Molly, whom she had connected with in unanticipated ways. Though her time in our class was relatively brief, she touched everyone in our room. Most of all, she has been taken from her parents, who stand at the front of the church next to the casket, thanking each person for coming, but with lifeless expressions on their faces.

We had not yet found the perfect way to help Emily communicate what she was feeling or what she was thinking. Did she remember what life was like previously? Did this new world feel like a second chance, or like a prison in which she was wheeled around and we did our best to guess what she wanted?

I learned later from the family that multiple bee stings put her body into anaphylactic shock. The first EpiPen did some good when it was eventually administered, but a person as allergic as Emily needed that first shot immediately and more advanced medical care right away. I was with Molly in the Polar Bear exhibit during these events, but the burden of guilt hangs heavily on me. Was there more I could have done had I been there?

I step into the long line of those waiting to say their good-byes to Emily. I see Jan enter the funeral home, and she joins me at the back of the line. "How are you doing, Jan? Hello, Bob." Bob was Jan's husband, whom I had met on a few previous occasions. Jan's eyes were puffy and red. It was clear she had been crying in the car.

"It is just so unreal," Jan says mournfully. "I am so sad, Michael. Never before have I felt so shocked and brokenhearted. When I finally have slept these past two nights, the only dreams I have involve Emily gasping for breaths, and us trying to call you, and the phone not working."

Her comments cut me real deep. This is like nothing I have ever felt or imagined. The tragedy makes my body ache, and food makes me gag. But I know what Jan is talking about. We were there. We all have our own last image of Emily.

Her husband Bob pulls her close and presses her forehead to his chest.

I look toward the casket and see some eighth-grade girls who must have been Emily's classmates in seventh grade last year before the accident. They are crying inconsolably.

We get to the front of the line. I shake hands with Mr. and Mrs. Thompkins and Emily's younger brother and tell them how sorry I am. Ms. Thompkins' eyes remain averted as I shake her weak hand.

I turn from the family and step forward to Emily's casket. I look and see Emily's eyes closed, her expression peaceful. Makeup has been applied to her face, and she is wearing clothes that are more fashionable than what she had typically worn to school these last few months. She looks like any typical teenager. I realize it's time to say my final words to her.

"Emily, I'm so sorry. I am so sorry that I didn't do more that day for you." I pause, not sure what else to say. I look at her sandy brown hair, which is parted on the right side, the ends of her hair stylishly flipped upwards. "We all miss you, Emily. You did so much for everyone, I'm just sorry we didn't get to know you more." I want to say "sorry" as much as I can, though I know that apologizing again and again won't make the slightest bit of difference. I can't think of anything else to say, so I just look down and whisper, "Goodbye, Emily."

I turn and walk toward the reception hall. I hear Jan crying loudly and Bob murmuring words of consolation.

*   *   *   *

The alarm goes off at five-thirty, my normal Monday wakeup time. Mr. Ballamy worked with district officials to give the students and staff of our classroom that Friday off. It is Monday morning now, though, and I didn't put in for a personal day, so I am slated to go to work. I was tossing and turning all night. Thankfully, I didn't dream about Emily as Jan said she had, but I don't know if I could have totaled more than two or three hours of sleep. Since I hit the snooze button so many times, I only have thirty minutes to get out of bed and get ready for work, but I can't seem to will myself to get out of bed. So I just lie there.

The alarm breaks the silence again. I hit the button one last time and roll over to look at the wall with bloodshot eyes. Suddenly the phone rings. It is the school's number, so I pick it up. It is our secretary.

"Hi, Jill." I am slightly embarrassed by how raspy my words sound.

"Hi, Michael. Mr. Ballamy asked me to give you a call and see if you were coming in." She pauses and reads my lack of response well. I am thankful for it. "Michael, I'm just going to tell him that you aren't coming in."

"Thank you, Jill," I say with sincerity. "I think I'm going to try to talk to some people today and tomorrow. Is it okay if I come in on Wednesday?"

She encourages me not to worry about work and says she will arrange a sub. I thank her one last time, hang up, and roll over. This time my eyes close as I turn, and fatigue finally overtakes my body. I stay in a dreamless sleep for the next five hours.

When I awake, I hope the waves of depression and anxiety won't totally engulf me.

CHAPTER FIFTEEN

I CALL PASTOR TIM later around noon, and we set up an appointment for tomorrow. After four o'clock, I phone Mr. Ballamy and confirm with him that I will be back to school on Wednesday. I apologize profusely for not being there for others at this time when I should be, as the teacher. He completely dismisses my concerns, though, and says there are more important things to take care of right now. "You need to be ready and right yourself, then come back and give your best to those kids."

I thank him sincerely, then he astonishes me by what he says next—"Besides, they have a pretty good substitute teacher over there in classroom A113. If you're not careful, there might not be an open teaching position to come back to."

I can tell he is ribbing me, so I give a small chuckle and ask him who the sub is.

"Me, of course!" he says. "The kids love me! That Stevie—oh, boy, what a hoot. He keeps trying to pick up my cell phone and have a conversation with me. I finally gave in at the end of the day, and we talked for like five minutes about chocolate cake."

Wow, people can be remarkable. I don't think Mr. Ballamy even knew Stevie's name before this week, and now they are having phone conversations in the classroom? I thank my principal and tell him I'd see him on Wednesday. I feel my first small glimmer of hopefulness since the zoo trip, which at the moment feels as desperately needed as oxygen.

$$*\qquad *\qquad *\qquad *$$

I usually don't go out on school nights—well, actually, almost never—but I need a friend. I call Dallas, and he tells me that Cindy said she would be able to hold down the fort at home. We decide to meet up at Boston Beer Works, a favorite hangout spot of ours ever since Dallas first moved to Boston. I arrive first and wait for him at one of the circular bar tables. I glance up at the closest TV screen and see that the Sox are playing the Yankees with the teams' two aces going up against each other. Usually this would be my focus, my topic of conversation, even with Dallas who couldn't care less, but today all of that seems pointless. It almost felt like a betrayal to watch the game and pretend things are normal so soon after losing Emily.

I see Dallas enter, wearing his blue-and-black North Face jacket. I stand and wave my hand to get his attention, and he ambles over and gives me a big bear-hug. For some reason I've never been terribly comfortable with hugs, but this feels good, and I appreciate Dallas for doing it. After a couple of pats on the shoulder, we sit down, and a waitress comes over to take our order. After a brief silence, Dallas gets right to the point and asks how I'm doing.

"To be honest, really bad, man. I've never had to face a death like this. I mean, my grandpa, who I loved, died when I was in high school, but that was different. He was in his eighties. I just don't know how to process Emily's death."

Dallas stares down at the table and slowly shakes his head as I speak. "It also bothers me, Dallas, that in the midst of this tragedy I am still thinking about myself in some ways. Like, not most of the time. Most of the time I think about Emily, her parents and her little brother. I think about them a lot. Yet I do wonder what's around the corner for me, because of everything that happened."

The waitress appears with our two dark porters, which we begin to sip slowly. "What are you most worried about that you think is around the corner?" Dallas asks me. "Are you not sure if you can bounce back from something like this?"

"To tell you the truth, Dallas, I'm worried about the legal aspect and how everything is going to play out. There was a substitute nurse, and she administered the EpiPen, but wasn't it ultimately my responsibility as the classroom teacher to call 911 and get Emily into the hands of EMTs as quickly as possible? If I had cell reception and had gotten there sooner, would she still be alive? Would I have recognized that something was wrong with Emily faster than the sub nurse? It's just not good, man, and I don't know if I'm in serious trouble. And I feel ashamed for even thinking about myself when the only thing that really matters is that an amazing girl lost her life, and a family that was just beginning to recover has been devastated again. I mean, how do you survive the death of your child?"

I take a deep breath, partially because I feel as though I have been talking a while, but also because it doesn't seem like there's anything left to say after pouring out all the guilty feelings that have been churning inside me since the accident.

"Mike," Dallas says, "I wish I could give more insight into the legal side of things, but I don't have any expertise in that area. I guess the only I advice I can give you is to try your best to only focus on what you can control, and to reach out to others for help. Those are big questions, and you should talk to your principal tomorrow. I don't know what the worst-case scenario is, but you know that I have your back, and your family has your back, and I'm sure all your friends and coworkers do, too."

After a long pause, Dallas starts talking in the fast-paced way he does when an idea comes to him—"Remember, Mikey, when we would give each other advice on girls during freshman year of high school? You told me to follow around Katie to let her know that I was interested. *Don't talk to her, just follow her around as much as possible until she notices you.* That was your advice! We really were the blind leading the blind back then when it came to girls, huh?" I gave a small smile, remembering our 'words of wisdom.' "Well," he continues, "that didn't work out so well. Katie just thought I was a weirdo stalker." He looks off and shakes his head, then takes a big gulp of his porter. The white foam coalesces around the side of the glass, then slowly slides back down. "You gave awful advice back then, Mike, like, *truly* awful."

"Thanks," I respond drily.

"But, you know, it's kind of the same thing now. I wish I had some great advice to give, but I don't. I think it would still be like back in high school with the blind leading the blind, you know?"

I stare at the ground, nodding along to what he is saying. My mind is partly listening, and partly in a dream-like fog.

"But, Mike, I'm here for you. We can sit and talk or not talk, or, heck since we're at a sports bar, we can even watch the game. I'm just trusting, man, that things are going to work out in the right way."

I look over at Dallas and make eye contact. "Thanks, man, I really appreciate it." I take another sip, then tilt my pint glass toward him. "Well, honestly, I don't think I can possibly turn down this once-in-a-lifetime offer from you to offer to watch a ball game, so I guess I vote for that."

Dallas smiles, and we both turn our eyes to the screen just in time to see Johnny Gomes hit a scorching line drive that barely clears the Green Monster. I give a half-hearted high-five to Dallas as raucous shouts and cheers erupt around us. Dallas swivels his head around, trying to get comfortable in this unfamiliar sports environment. "So, is what's-his-face still on the team? Nomar?"

For the first time since the accident I laugh. "Sorry, Dallas, Nomar left, like, eight years ago."

"Well, crap, that was the one guy I knew."

"It's all right. Good effort." Even though I know we'll be watching the rest of the game mostly in silence, it feels good not being alone right now.

CHAPTER SIXTEEN

THE FIRST DAY BACK is rough. Emotionally I know I don't have much to give, though Stevie makes the transition back a whole lot easier. "Hii, Miiisster Sniff!" rings out his familiar and much-appreciated greeting.

"Hey, Stevie, good to see you. I sure missed you guys."

"Hiii, Miiister Sniiiiiff!" he says with even more emphasis than usual on his "i's." Just seeing Stevie and the other students breaks through some sort of invisible wall I couldn't breach on my own at home. I know the heavy feelings of sadness will return, but for now this place and these kids are giving me the respite I need.

"Hey, Stevie, it is really good to see you and the rest of the class. Why don't you put your bag away, and then we can talk about your day over the phone, okay?"

"Oo-kay!" Stevie exclaims, and walks toward the closet. Molly follows Stevie, and she is making vocalizations, showing that her anxiety is already pretty high.

"Hi, Molly," I say while extending my closed hand to give her a fist-bump without all the sensory input of a full-blown high-five. She is looking up toward the ceiling but still reaches out and manages to connect knuckles with me, giving me a nice greeting. Her gaze is still skyward as she stays in place, rocking slightly.

Finally, she starts pointing toward the back of the room. "Emily, Emily," she repeats. Like when a DVD case or the classroom trash can is out of place, Molly recognizes something is not right. Her rocking intensifies.

My heart sinks. She's asking where her friend is. My eyes start to fill, but I keep it together. "I'm sorry, Molly. Emily won't be coming back. Do you miss your friend?"

"Yes, yes," Molly answers with a higher-pitched intonation.

A lump forms in my throat. "I'm so sorry, Molly," I say again, this time trying my best to keep my emotions in check. Molly and Emily had such a special friendship—one that brought out the best in each of them. So many kids, and adults, long for what they had. I turn my back, because this time a tear does end up rolling down my cheek. These next couple of days will be rough. I am not sure how we as a class should grieve for our classmate and friend.

*   *   *   *

Mr. Ballamy calls me into his office. I have taken my anxiety medication to take an edge off my nerves, but they're still present. Typically, Mr. Ballamy's leadership style is similar to one of those old-school coaches—you know, the type who wouldn't allow water-breaks during practice for fear it would make his players soft. However, after our last conversation, my mindset has been altered. Before I sit down, I earnestly thank him for covering my class. He acknowledges my gratitude with a stoic look on his face and says he did what he was supposed to do as a principal—make sure his staff and students were supported in every way possible.

Mr. Ballamy goes on to tell me that he knows how things unfolded by reading the police report. He doesn't need any more specifics, at least for right now. "I called you in, Michael, because I just wanted to see how you were doing and to tell you how very sorry I am."

I look up at him, surprised. I see moisture is beginning to form in the eyes of "The General." He pauses for a moment, sliding his thumb and forefinger under his wire rimmed glasses.

"I know that I don't visit your class as much as I should," he says. "I wish I had gotten to know Emily more. She was a part of my school, part of Twin Oaks. Her loss reminds me of my own fourth-grade nephew who passed away—oh, how long ago was that? I guess almost seven years now."

I didn't know any of this about Mr. Ballamy's past. He's not the type who shares much about his personal life. "Life just doesn't make sense sometimes," he says. I nod. After a long pause, he drops some unsettling news: "Michael, the Thompkins family is going to sue the school district."

I immediately get a sick feeling in my stomach as the scenario on which I speculated with Dallas becomes a reality. "Oh, man, that is not good," is all I can muster for a reply.

Mr. Ballamy goes on to say that he was surprised when he called Ms. Thompkins that she wasn't angry with him or me, or even the substitute nurse. Her anger was directed at the school district. She felt that they didn't take her daughter's medical condition seriously and didn't have a clear enough medical plan laid out to give to subs for field trips. She asserted that a properly trained backup nurse should have been secured within the first week of school for situations like this. With an anguished tone, Ms. Thompkins confided that these were the fears she fought against before re-enrolling her daughter at school, and now her daughter was dead.

Mr. Ballamy shakes his head slowly and gives a heavy sigh. "It breaks my heart, because this poor mother is putting part of the blame on herself, even if she didn't say it in so many words. She started sobbing on the phone, and there was nothing I could say. I wanted to let her know that I've felt loss, too, not like hers, but my nephew's death tore me up." He continues, his voice becomes more intense, "And if it had been due to negligence in any way"—he pounds his fist on the desk—"I would have wanted to string up someone's back end, too!"

My head snaps up from its bowed position. I can see him taking deep breaths and trying to reel in his emotions. In a controlled voice he says, "But I know I represent the district, so I told Ms. Thompkins that she should do what she feels is best, and just left it at that." I can tell the difficult conversation still weighs heavily on my principal. As he stares out his office window, I get the sense that he wishes he had said more to Ms. Thompkins, but was at a loss because he didn't know what the right words would have been.

"Things might get a little tough, but Special Ed administration and our district lawyer will be walking through the process with us. I will do my best to support you in any way I can. Your focus needs to be on your kids and that classroom." As he talks, he clenches both fists and thrusts them forward to emphasize the point to stay focused on the kids. "Taking care of your class includes yourself and your staff too." My mind and heart are racing, but I move my head up and down. "My job as administrator is to take any hits coming our school's way," he says.

I wonder how this could be the same guy I thought was detached and cold for so long. The memory of him forgetting to order our class T-shirts seems like forever ago. He was understanding of the family's need for justice and didn't view them as the enemy, and was also willing to put his own neck on the line in case the district blamed us for not being proactive enough. I leave the meeting with even more admiration for Mr. Ballamy. He may not be warm, or pat you on the back for the small stuff, but he's a good man, and I vow never to speak ill of him ever again. Anyone willing to lay down his reputation, or even his career, for those under him is worthy of respect. Perhaps the nickname "General" is more appropriate than I realized.

*   *   *   *

I dismiss my class a couple of minutes early to beat the rush of kids headed to the cafeteria for lunch. I had received the following email late Sunday night, and I decided life was too short to keep closing off people or avoiding conversations because of the possible anxiety that could ensue. I open Sunday's email and read it again before heading over to Ms. Liu's classroom:

> *Hi Michael,*
>
> *I would have called, but I didn't have your number. I just wanted to express how heartbroken I am about Emily. If you need a friend to talk to, or if you just want to have a quiet lunch together, please know that my door is always open. Thinking about you and your class.*
>
> *Sincerely,*
> *Josie*

Even her written communication has a dulcet tone. Maybe it's just the way we read the emails from the people we care about, but I believe it's more—you can feel the warmth in her writing. I put my computer into sleep mode and head out to her classroom.

*   *   *   *

I walk to Ms. Liu's class with my water bottle and sack lunch and peer through the edge of the glass window. I see all twenty-eight of her students, heads down, busily writing away. Josie sees me out of the corner of her eye, turns, and gives me her side-smile. I detect something different, however. Concern? I smile back and mouth, "Can we talk at lunch?" while holding my brown bag aloft. It hits me that she probably can't lip-read my question, and my suspicion is confirmed when she mouths an exaggerated "What?" I grin and shrug.

Josie holds up her index finger, indicating class will be dismissed in just a minute. She gains the students' attention with one single hand-raise. "All right, class, great sustained silent writing. Have a good lunch, and don't forget to complete your homework on *To Kill a Mockingbird*. Remember, the essay should include an interpretation of the quote: 'Mockingbirds don't do one thing but make music for us to enjoy . . . but sing their hearts out for us. That's why it's a sin to kill a mockingbird.' And *just* as a reminder, I want this to be *your* opinion and explanation, and not a copy-and-paste job from Sparknotes."

I see a couple of boys in the back of the class glance over at each other nervously.

"I have seen every idea that website has to offer just by reading plagiarized student essays from last year," she switches to a somewhat playful, pleading tone, "so please, please don't be that student!"

After a few small chuckles from the class, she changes to her no-nonsense voice. "But, seriously, don't be the one who makes me have to call your parents and give you a zero."

She makes the last comment while looking directly at one of the boys in the back who flashed a guilty look earlier. I'm impressed by the way Ms. Liu can convey that she means what she says, but with a light-handed touch. She closes with, "Okay, have a nice lunch, everyone!" as the lunch bell rings and the kids frantically shove their Harper Lee paperbacks and homework notebooks into their backpacks.

The students shuffle out the door, saying goodbyes to Ms. Liu. Some peer tutors spot me and say, "Hi, Mr. Smith," or smile and wave as they exit. With the classroom quiet and empty, my mind turns to the events of last week, and I see Josie has a reflective look on her face as well.

She grabs her lunch bag with a classy floral design out of her bottom desk drawer and sets it on one of the student desks near the front of the room. "Should we just eat in here?"

I let her know that is my preference, and I pull a second student chair across from hers.

"So how are you holding up, Michael?"

"I'm hanging in there, I think. Everything feels surreal. Like, being here with the kids feels so normal it almost doesn't seem right." I start to unpack my not-atypical lunch of a peanut-butter sandwich, apple, chips, and Gushers. When I look over at Josie's whole-wheat tortilla wrap with hummus, lettuce and feta and her plain yogurt with fresh blueberries, I have to smile at the dissimilarity of our packed lunches.

Josie's eyes light up as she spots the Gushers, and she gives a thumbs-up. "My mom never let me have those growing up."

I tear open the bag and offer her a piece, which she pops into her mouth without hesitation. We eat in silence for a while, and then I decide it's time to try to open up a little.

"Josie, can I ask you a question?"

She takes a bite of her wrap and indicates that it is okay.

"Do you feel like just going about the school day as if nothing happened is dishonoring Emily's memory?" I stammer on trying to finish my question. "I mean, what is the right way to act? The kids in the class know something is wrong, but I don't know how to talk to them about what has happened. I mean, do you talk about death with someone who may not have the ability to understand what that means?" I think of Molly, who was pointing and communicating that Emily was not there and something was wrong, and my deficient response to her. "It just doesn't seem fair to give half-true answers to friends like Molly, and then each day act more and more as if nothing has happened."

"Hmmm," Josie thought for a second, "I'm not sure there is a right or easy answer to that." Her thin, black eyebrows are knitted together. "You're trying to figure out what the right thing is to say to your students, and not just pretend like your time with Emily didn't exist. What would be respectful of her is your question, right?"

"Yeah, exactly," I say, then take a few bites of my plain sandwich.

"Well, I'm no expert, but I think you need to let your students know that Emily has passed away and that she is not coming back. I think it's okay to let the kids know what you are feeling, too—acknowledging that you are sad for Emily, her family, her friends, and that you are feeling sad yourself." She pauses to gather her thoughts. "If you are unable to grieve and feel sad, I think you just build up walls that won't let you be there for others who are also grieving. I guess I see it as it's always better to feel something, even if it's painful, than to push it all down and try not to feel anything at all."

"So how do you deal with hard things like this, Josie?" I ask, leaning forward.

Josie thinks for a moment before responding. I like the way she is circumspect in expressing her thoughts, but she never seems paralyzed with finding the right words, as I sometimes find myself to be.

"I guess for me it's reaching out and talking with my closest friends," she says. "I'm not one who likes to share with a bunch of other people, but I always feel better after talking to my friends from Brown. They will listen without judging and share their honest opinions. That's always meant a lot to me." Then, as if remembering that she probably should include her boyfriend in the discussion of people she talks to, she adds, "I talk to Bobby over the phone, too. He's good at listening."

I don't really feel like talking about her boyfriend Bobby, so I focus more on her friends from college. "That's really great that you still keep in touch with your college girlfriends. I have a buddy like that who I can talk to from high school, but, yeah, a lot of times conversations with people can be really hard for me in general." I get a sick feeling and regret making that last statement, as I feel I may have revealed a bit too much of my own problems to my co-worker.

Josie just smiles and puts my racing mind at ease. "It's okay, Michael. I pegged you as a little more of an introvert, like me, but it's good to get out of your classroom sometimes. The other day we were talking about awkward middle-school moments, and although *technically* you weren't in middle school, I had to share your story about taking out your fourth-grade teacher while playing basketball and sending her to the hospital. That got an especially good laugh out of Mr. Johnson with the giant gray mustache. I still can't believe how huge that thing is . . . it's . . . it's incredible!"

I laugh. Mr. Johnson did have a large mustache, but I never heard someone talk about it such reverent tones before.

"Sometimes I want to just reach out and tug the end of it. Is that weird?"

I throw my head back, laughing at Josie's comments—forgetting for a moment the suffocating weight on my heart. "Yes, Josie, that is definitely weird. I would recommend *never* sharing that with Mr. Johnson."

Josie's eyes are twinkling. "I like when you throw your head back and laugh. I'd say it's almost as unique as Mr. Johnson's—" She doesn't finish her sentence, but instead holds her pointer-finger horizontally above her upper lip. Who would have known Josie was so quirky? In a good way, though. You would never guess it if you just saw her teaching, or in meetings, or during brief interactions in the hallways.

Suddenly, the two-minute warning lunch bell rings. We both look down at our barely-eaten lunches and laugh. Talking took priority over eating for me for once. "Thanks,

Josie, I needed to laugh again," I say. "Thanks for listening, too. I really appreciate it."

Josie gives a slight smile, then switches easily from goofy to serious. "I'm glad you came in, too, Michael. I'll keep thinking about how to approach walking your kids through this tough time. I know you are the right person to do it, though."

I can hear her students outside the classroom door, so I toss my half-eaten sandwich back into my lunch-sack. As I get up, Josie says kindly, "I can always save you a seat in the teachers' lounge, you know."

"Yeah, I will honestly try to go," I say seriously as I head toward the door, "as long as you don't stare at you-know-who too much." I put up a finger moustache this time. Josie laughs, and for some reason I am not second-guessing myself as I normally do during conversations. I move past the the crowd of students who are pressing toward her door and realize I went a whole conversation without getting fixated on eye contact, or even breaking into profuse sweating.

As I approach my door, I hear the familiar shuffle of Justin's feet coming around the corner of the hallway and Barbara and Stevie laughing together about something that happened at lunch. I don't know what these next couple months will be like, but I know it's good to be here.

*   *   *   *

My lunchtime conversation with Josie reminds me of an old speech by Coach Jim Valvano, a championship-winning college basketball coach who accepted an award for courage just eight weeks before cancer took his life at age forty-seven.

During his speech at the ESPN award show, he said, "If you laugh, you think, and you cry, that's a full day. That's a heck of a day. You do that seven days a week, you're going to have something special." He said all of that while staring down death, which he must have known was no longer knocking, but pounding at his door.

His story and his words lived on past that night and his death. In fact, those inspirational words may be more of his legacy than his underdog 1983 NCAA tournament championship run. Jimmy V. chose to appreciate and enjoy every moment of his life until the very end. *The laughs and the cries,* I think.

CHAPTER SEVENTEEN

THE FIRST FULL WEEK back at school, I come in feeling like a broken version of myself, but—as is so often the case with the kids in our classroom—they help put me back together again. I may produce a genuine smile at a funny moment, or get excited when Stevie counts to 20 and only misses the number 13. The old cliché, "Kids give you so much more than you could ever give them," never feels more true than now, after that first week back in our class.

It is the last hour before the weekend, and Devonte is reciting some of his favorite baseball statistics out loud. Stacey, one of the peer tutors from Ms. Liu's class, overhears the number-filled monologue and asks excitedly, "Wow, Devonte, how do you know all of that?" Devonte looks at the source of the interruption for a second, and then carries on with his recitation. I am impressed with Stacey's persistence, though, as she continues to try to engage with him.

"No, Devonte, that is really cool!" Stacey says. "My little brother, Luke, is in sixth grade, and he loves talking about baseball. He says everyone else in his grade is into basketball or football. He would love talking about the Red Sox with you!" She swivels in her chair from Devonte to me and asks, "Can I bring him in here sometime?"

It takes me a second to realize the conversation has shifted to me. My anxiety response kicks into high gear. "I'm sorry. What did you say?" Blotches of warm sweat pool up in all of my least favorite places. Stacey repeats her question, and my body heat pushes higher. As sweat begins to coat my forehead and forearms, I want to retreat to the bathroom and begin my mental checklist of reassuring phrases and mantras. Instead, I hear the calm voice of Dr. Givens and picture the graph she had drawn about riding out a wave of anxiety. I need to learn how to do this.

I push forward in the conversation, as if I had no perspiration percolating up to my skin's surface. "That would be great if your brother was able to join us," I say in a hopefully enthusiastic way. The sweating persists to the point where it starts to drip. I go to the Kleenex box, grab a couple of tissues, and give my forehead and arms a good swipe. I don't abort the conversation, though, and I let her know I could write a note right now that she could give to her brother's teacher. Unfortunately, the barrage of negative thoughts that always goes hand-in-hand with such moments has begun: *What's Stacey thinking about why I'm sweating so much? She isn't going to want to come back and help out in the classroom now. What's the matter wi—*

Then, suddenly, I move on. I don't try to fight the thoughts or use a positive affirmation. I just move on. I know that the negative chatter will eventually stop, and so will the sweating.

I take another swipe with the tissue, write the note for Luke's teacher, and hand it to Stacey. As she takes the note and heads out the door, I feel a strange sense of accomplishment. I am less focused on the dampness of my undershirt, and thinking about the present once again. It definitely wasn't an anxiety-free interchange, but it was a victory, because I endured the sweat-laced conversation without retreating, and it ended without my typical web of anxious thoughts and feelings of shame. For at least this one moment, I proved I could ride out a wave of anxiety in the real world and it would all be okay in the end.

*   *   *   *

Devonte pretty much meets his favorite person in the world the following Monday. Luke comes in with a sports-card binder clutched to his chest. He asks me if he can show it to Devonte. I say, "Of course!" The two of them talk for twenty minutes straight about the rows of ballplayers organized and tucked away into the plastic sheets that make up Luke's collection. Luke tells Devonte the story behind each card, and why that player made the cut for being in his book of favorite baseball cards. Devonte listens and makes the best eye contact I have ever seen from him. He also blows Luke away with his knowledge of stats.

About ten minutes into their conversation, Luke starts to test Devonte with questions like, "How many hits did Johnny Damon have in 2004?" or "How many strikeouts did Pedro Martinez have in 1999?" Devonte gets them all correct! "That is unbelievable!" Luke shouts in amazement after Devonte lists off all of Tim Wakefield's 2007 statistics. "I've never met anyone who knows sports as well as you!"

Devonte looks straight ahead, seeming not to hear Luke's compliment or awestruck tone of voice. Luke gently rubs his finger over the plastic protection holding his Tim Wakefield card. "Devonte, this card is actually probably my very favorite of all of them." He pauses as if building up dramatic suspense. "Even though Tim Wakefield isn't the best player, I got it the day my dad took me to my first game at Fenway Park. It was a playoff game, and Tim Wakefield pitched that day. He only gave up one run in seven innings. That was the year they won the World Series! Isn't that cool, Devonte?"

"Yes," Devonte says with his typical monotone voice and flat affect. If you didn't know better, you might think this conversation bored him, but I knew he was loving it. Small clues like his eyes focusing more on the person he was talking to revealed his true feelings, and if you looked closely you could see the corners of his mouth twitch, as if trying to fight off a smile.

Luke is thrilled to have someone to talk baseball with. He replays the events of his first Sox game. "Every time the A's tried to hit Wakefield, they looked like this—" Luke stands up and crouches, holding an imaginary bat as if waiting for the pitch. He takes a huge exaggerated swing, feigns frustration, then looks back as if the ball is lodged in the catcher's mitt. He laughs and exalts, "You wouldn't believe how lost those players looked trying to hit that knuckleball!"

They talk for a few more minutes, but eventually I have to remind Luke that it is time for him to head back to class. I think if I didn't interfere, Luke would have been content to stay all day talking baseball with Devonte. He gives Devonte a high-five and says, "See you on Friday." He then turns toward me to confirm. "Mrs. Tanner said I can come twice a week—could I come into your guys' class Mondays and Fridays?" I told him that was fine with me. "All right! Cool! See you then, Devonte. I'll bring more cards on Friday!"

Devonte not only reciprocates the high-five earlier but also imitates Luke's good-bye and repeats, "See you on Friday." After Luke leaves, Devonte turns his attention back to his math worksheet. This time, however, the twitching corners of his mouth transform into a full smile. Devonte has made a true friend outside of our classroom.

*   *   *   *

I stay late catching up on the emails, paperwork and lesson plans that piled up from the three days of work I missed. As I drive home at seven o'clock, I am thinking about Molly. She has been more agitated since that day at the zoo. It pains me to know she is both hurt and confused.

I think back to my conversation with Josie about grieving. I know the more typical approach of "talking it out" won't be a meaningful way for Molly, or any of our students, to process their grief and remember Emily. I then picture Emily, and reflect on who she was, her story, her life and impact on others, and suddenly an idea starts to form.

At home I pull out my laptop and open up my school email. I find Josie's old email from last Sunday and hit 'Reply.'

"Dear Josie, I hope you are doing well," I begin. "I was thinking about what you and I talked about on Wednesday, and was wondering what you thought about this idea . . ."

CHAPTER EIGHTEEN

"HI MR. SMITH. IS it okay for us to come in?"

I wave Ms. Liu's kids in to join us. Folding chairs are placed in three rows of eight facing the front of the room. Cory has already come in and is sitting next to Justin, giving him repeated small high-fives to keep him engaged. Jan is beside Molly at the end of the second row. Though I know Molly's anxiety levels are heightened by this change in her daily routine, the environment, and all the new people entering our classroom, I still strongly feel it is the right thing to do. Some of us had an opportunity to say good-bye to Emily at the wake, but her classmates and the peer tutors didn't get that chance. That being said, however, Molly is having a really hard time, making loud vocalizations and rocking back and forth in her seat to try to calm herself.

Luke has already come in and is sitting next to his new baseball buddy. Devonte looks pleased. As the rest of Ms. Liu's students shuffle into the classroom, I notice some of the kids are already tearing up. Stacey, Luke's older sister, looks as if she started crying well before entering the classroom, her eyes puffy and nose red at the tip. She enters with her head down, clutching a wad of tissues, and sits by Stephanie. To Stephanie's right sits another of the girl peer tutors who always seemed to gravitate toward her and would compliment Stephanie on her outfits.

One of the eighth-grade boys, Derek, claims a seat next to Stevie. He greets Stevie with, "What's up?" and introduces him to his friend Sam. Sam has never been in our classroom before, but Stevie is the ultimate greeter. He reaches out his hand for a high-five and says, "Hiiii, Sammmm!" Stevie loves to meet new people, and he has a big grin on his face.

Sam smiles, but looks uncertainly at Derek, who shoves him in the arm and says, "Don't leave Stevie hangin', man! Give him a high-five!"

Sam apologizes and stretches out his arm to slap Stevie's palm. With that simple interaction you can see Sam's discomfort begin to disappear.

The last of Ms. Liu's students come in and fill in the remaining empty seats or take up positions in the back of the room. This fills our class to capacity. I think about Rachael Thompkins' email in which she wrote that she wouldn't be able to attend today's remembrance of Emily because the feelings were too raw.

Earlier in the day, Jill, our school secretary, called the classroom and told me Ms. Thompkins had dropped off a couple of pictures but had left immediately afterwards. Though we didn't get to talk, I am thankful that she gave her approval for the classroom ceremony, and that she thought it was important enough to provide the pictures of her daughter.

There are two 8x10s in simple silver frames. Judging by the date stamp on the first image, it was taken three years ago, when Emily was in fifth grade. She was outside playing with three other girls. Emily had her arms around two of them, although the face of the girl on the left couldn't be fully seen because her head was thrown back in laughter. The other girl is beaming a brace-filled smile. The fourth girl is in the background doing a cartwheel, and the photo captures the action perfectly, as her body is practically perpendicular to the green grass. It is a cheery, carefree photo. The second photo is a black and white close-up of Emily's face, taken two weeks before the zoo trip. She has an expression that approximates a smile, but her eyes look distant.

The two photos are both Emily. She lived both lives, and was both people. I believe both images show a person of equal worth. However, the pictures have a conspicuous difference. Staring at the photo of her as a ten-year-old is heartbreaking, as it represents all of the things she couldn't do after the first devastating incident almost two years ago. I later learn that it was at the house of the girl who is laughing so hard in the photo where the first bee sting occurred. Her parents offered typical care for it, not knowing the severity of her allergies until it was too late. How sad and frightening for her friend. Would that girl ever have that hearty, joyful laugh again?

It is all too sad, and I feel my eyes start to water as I make my way from the back of the room toward the front to start our time of saying goodbye to Emily—to give everyone, especially my students, a way to remember their friend and a chance to grieve.

*   *   *   *

Before starting our time of remembrance, I take one more quick inventory of the room. Emily touched so many people, many of whom I don't recognize. It has to be the most full this room has ever been. The noise-level is also quite high— not from all the students and adults that fill the chairs and line the walls, but mainly from Molly, whose vocalizations are increasing in pitch and volume. Every thirty seconds or so, Stephanie looks over at Molly and says in a maternal voice, "It's okay, Molly, it's okay."

I'm starting to feel bad. Molly was one of the main students I hoped would find some comfort from this gathering, but by inviting so many people and changing her world so much, did I set her up for a meltdown? She will reach her threshold soon, and her rocking and vocalizations will escalate into yelling and fist-pounding. I decide that if it gets to that level I will ask Jan to take Molly into the halls to walk and hopefully bring her to a more regulated state.

I am about to welcome everyone and begin the program when Mr. Ballamy enters. I nod at him, hoping to convey my appreciation of his presence. He nods back at me, and then at Ms. Liu, who stands by the side wall of the classroom nearest the door. She walks to the principal, and he gives her a big side-hug. Stevie gets up, runs over and shouts, "Hi Mr. Baaammeee!" He gives Stevie a friendly smile and fist-pound, then politely gestures for him to return to his seat.

I take a deep breath, exhale slowly, and then begin. "Emily was a special girl whom we were all fortunate to have in our lives. She joined our class midway through the year, so she had only been in our class for a little over three months. I don't know why, but I have found that sometimes the most life-shaping people or moments often take place during the briefest of seasons. I know all of us in the room, who were lucky enough to get to know Emily during our short time with her, would say they were better people for having known her.

"If you don't mind, I'd like to share a few examples. I remember watching in awe as Emily connected with Stephanie and the two of them would listen to music together. That was a special day for me, because I remember how you, Stephanie"—I pause and gesture toward Stephanie—"showed Emily how to use her voice with a switch to tell us that she liked the same song that you did." I smile again toward Stephanie, who has her head down and is staring into her lap.

I continue. "I remember how Emily connected with many of the peer tutors who are here today. Two of the girls up front, Chelsea and Rosa, would come in and used to read stories with her almost every other day. She really enjoyed those times of just being with you girls." Tears stream down Chelsea's face. "Emily always seemed extra alert after you guys read a *Twilight* book together."

I look at Molly this time. She is still rocking and making sounds that are mostly strings of vowels, but she is laughing periodically, too, which makes me think she is probably replaying something in her mind that is funny to her. It's okay, even if Molly doesn't comprehend all I'm saying; it's still important for the words to be said. "Molly, I think you and Emily had a particularly special connection, even starting that first day she came into our class. You looked calmer than I had ever seen you before when you were with Emily, and Emily always looked happy when she was spending time with you. I remember the first time you gave Emily a high-five with Nurse Nancy helping support her arm. After that day, you would initiate those high-fives—with Emily, no one else. I think Emily knew that was special, Molly."

I try to see if that recollection will help bring Molly back to the present and stop the images probably playing on loop in her mind. She is still, however, pretty deeply retreated into herself, but maybe it is helping her to cope. After a brief pause, I take a deep breath in, let it out, then nod my head. "That's pretty much what was on my heart. Is there anyone else who would like to say any words about Emily or share any good memories you had with her?"

Chelsea, who had been crying earlier, raises her hand. She faces the two framed photos that have been set up on a small desk at the front of the room, and speaks to them. "Emily, Rosa and I will miss reading with you. When I first came into the class, I didn't really know how to act or what to say, but after that first day I started to get it more. After a week I wasn't nervous anymore to come in. In fact, reading *Twilight* with you became one of the favorite parts of my week, and I told all my friends about you. I just wanted to let you know they are really sorry about what happened to you, and for your family too." With her final words of "I'm going to miss you," Chelsea begins to sob.

Jan raises her hand and says she would like to speak. "Emily, I think it is a testament to you that we have so many people here today. You made this big of a difference in just three months. You had a very gentle and kind heart, and I can tell by looking at that photo of you with your friends that you have always been that sweet, kind girl. Good-bye, love."

Two more girls from Ms. Liu's class speak. One, a weekly peer tutor, shares about how much it meant when Emily had said "hello" to her using her head and the Big Mac switch. The second girl, very tall and dressed in all black, I do not recognize. I am confused because I have never seen her come into the room, yet when she speaks it's as if she had a real history with Emily. The girl talks about how outgoing and friendly Emily was with everyone, not just with her friends. She loved playing stupid games like M.A.S.H. with her—

laughing hysterically when Emily would always get the mansion with her secret guy crush. "You were the luckiest M.A.S.H. player I have ever seen," she says with a touch of humor, but you can tell there is no laughter behind her words. I wonder who this girl is?

I look around to see if anyone else has any last words before I close. I glance over at Ms. Liu, who has a Kleenex out and is dabbing at the tears running down her cheeks. I ask Stephanie if she wants to say anything to or about Emily. She shakes her head and looks somber.

"Okay, well, let's just have a moment of silence to remember Emily." Molly seems to be barely hanging on, making loud humming noises as she continues to move back and forth in her chair. "I know it may not be a true moment of silence, but that's okay," I reassure everyone.

I don't know how or why things like this happen sometimes, but after I say, "To remember Emily," the whole room falls into complete silence. My eyes dart to Molly, who for the first time during this whole ceremony is sitting in her chair staring forward—absolutely silent. In fact, I hear none of the other sounds I've grown accustomed to in our classroom. For the next ten seconds, all are quietly thinking about Emily in their own way. The moment gives me chills.

"Thank you for teaching us so much in just three months, Emily," I conclude. "We will always remember you."

CHAPTER NINETEEN

IT'S MONDAY MORNING, AND the day's drama starts quickly. Stephanie comes in, and she is not happy. Apparently Stevie took her One Direction stuffed doll and threw it out the bus window on the way to school. When I hear the story, I accidentally let out a small laugh, but quickly cover it with a cough. I knew Devonte wasn't a fan of the band, but I guess this musical group was becoming quite the dividing force within our classroom.

I switch to my stern teacher voice, turn toward the offender, and say, "Stevie, that is not okay. What you did was not kind to Stephanie. Why did you do that?"

Stevie takes in a deep breath, almost exaggerates the exhale, then buries both hands and face into his lap. With the low muscle tone that comes with Down syndrome he falls into this posture easily. I do feel bad for Stephanie, though, who is currently giving Stevie a death stare as you might see from an old married woman whose spouse has forgotten their anniversary.

"Stevie," I tell him, "what do you need to say to Stephanie before we figure out how we are going to make this right?"

Stevie peers up from his lap. Big tears now cover his face. "I'm sa-sa-sorry, Mr. Snifff."

"No, Stevie, not to me, but to Stephanie. It was her doll you threw out the bus window."

"Sa-sorry, Steephanicee," Stevie says while lumbering up from his chair. He holds up his hand for a high-five, which he hopes will melt away any feelings of animosity. Stephanie's hard glare does not dissipate. Stevie tries one more time, turning up the charm, this time giving her a side hug and placing his head gently on her shoulder. "I'm sa-sorry Stephanieee. So sa-sa-sorry." With that, I can see the anger drain from Stephanie's face and body.

"It's okay, Stevie. Don't do that, though. Don't do that, okay?"

"I won't, Stephanieeee."

I know we have been working on high-fives over hugs all year long, but sometimes moments like these are just too special to break up. I can't help but think if everyone could heal their conflicts this quickly the world would be a substantially better place. In fact, the apology and pardon happened so fast I don't know if I need to say more. I decide that the misdeed warrants a little more follow-through, however, so I tell Stevie I will have to call his parents and he will need to buy Stephanie a new doll. His eyes start to well with tears; one breaks through and rolls down his cheek. With his mouth turned downward he silently bobs his head.

I call Stephanie over to my computer. We look online and find a doll like the one she had that is either lying forlornly on some asphalt or claimed happily by another One Direction fan. I order it and figure I'd pay for it or Stevie's parents would, if they offered. Either way, I think that is the least Stephanie deserves after her great display of forgiveness.

Barbara goes to the front of the classroom for the daily morning meeting. The class reviews the date, weather, attendance, schedule for the day, and any special announcements. I can hear the kids reciting, "Today is Wednesday, June 4th, 2012."

During the announcements Barbara informs the class, "Today, Devonte's friend, Luke, will be joining us for lunch," while smiling over at Devonte. I am in the back, printing out some final pictures I found online for our upcoming lesson, when suddenly the phone rings. Jan picks it up and says in a serious tone, "Oh, okay. Yes, he is right here."

I thank Jan and take the phone. "Hello, this is Mr. Smith."

"Hi, Mr. Smith. It's Rachael Thompkins. I'm sorry to be calling you when you have students, but I was wondering if we could talk?"

"Ms. Thompkins, hi . . . please, no apologies needed. Thank you for calling," I say with some surprise in my voice. I quickly follow with, "How are you doing?"

"I'm okay. Well, not really, but, you know . . . "

"Yeah." My voice lowers as I feel a stab of sorrow.

"I just wanted to call and say thank you, Mr. Smith."

"Thank you?" I reply, bewildered. "For what?"

"I have been meaning to call for a while, but it has just been too painful."

I assure her that there had been no expectation for her to call.

"Anyways," she continues, "I just had to share a story with you that I heard yesterday from one of my old girlfriends, Lisa. I actually hadn't talked to Lisa in at least four years. We used to love talking about *American Idol* and who we were rooting for each week. She was crushed when her guy David Archuleta was runner-up that season. Sorry, it feels like I'm rambling. Am I rambling? Are you sure that you don't need to get back to your class?" she asks considerately.

I assure her that she is not rambling, and that Jan and Barb will be able to start the morning lesson while we talk. Ms. Thompkins finds the response satisfactory, but says, "Okay, well, let me know when you need to go." I tell her I will, and I encourage her to go on.

"So," she continues, "Lisa's daughter, Vanessa, was a friend of Em's back when they were at the same elementary school. At that time they were inseparable—Vanessa was Emily's best friend, for sure. I think Vanessa spent the night at our house, or Emily at theirs, at least once a week. The summer after fourth grade, Lisa and her husband bought a house in a different part of the district, so Vanessa ended up moving to a different school. Emily was heartbroken at the time. They promised they would stay in touch forever, but, as things go, they both found new friends, and those weekend sleepovers started to become less and less frequent. Eventually the two girls just stopped hanging out."

I think back to that picture of Emily with her fifth-grade friends. I guess Vanessa had left the summer before that photo was taken.

"So, as I said," Ms. Thompkins continued, "Vanessa ended up going to a different elementary school, and she was far enough away from us that it also meant that she attended a different middle school as well. Emily was at Woodland Middle, while Vanessa came to Twin Oaks." She took an audible breath. Clearly this was not an easy story for her to tell.

"After the, um, accident, Emily missed quite a bit of school, as she was recovering. When she was well enough to return, the IEP team tried to stick Emily back at her old school in a program that had the same title as yours, but nothing about it resembled a classroom. When I observed the 'class' she was slated to go to, I couldn't believe it. There were only two kids, housed in a back portable that was furthest away from the rest of the school. When I came in, the students were just sitting there in the middle of the school day, barely attended to, as a Disney movie played in the background. I brought up my many concerns about what I saw at my first-ever IEP meeting, but it was like the people from the district didn't hear a thing I was saying. I remember being so angry and thinking, *Over my dead body will my daughter be placed in that class.* After multiple meetings, and preparing to go to mediation, the district said they had found a more appropriate placement for my daughter, which was at Twin Oaks.

"When Em finally started in your class in February, I think there was just too much on my mind, because I never put it together that her old friend, Vanessa, would be at the same school."

Ms. Thompkins pauses. I am unsure of what to say, but fortunately she continues on. I want her to shape the direction of this conversation, anyway.

"Back in fourth grade," she says, "Vanessa and Em were inseparable. But three years after the move, when the allergic reaction happened, the girls had already gone their separate ways a couple years prior. I had lost touch with Lisa, so neither one of them knew what had happened to Emily. Anyways, to make a long story short, last night Lisa called me for the first time in years and said that she was heartbroken and devastated about everything. She hadn't known about either accident." Ms. Thompkins pauses again, and when she resumes, her voice sounds noticeably different by what sounds like a huge lump in her throat. "It was weird. I sort of knew that I hadn't talked to Lisa since the accident last year, but at the same time I was somewhat offended that she had known absolutely nothing!"

"How did Lisa find out about—everything?" I ask Ms. Thompkins. I'm inquiring about Emily's passing, but can't bring myself to say the words.

"She learned about Emily's death from the letter Mr. Ballamy had written to all the parents explaining what had happened, and what a tragic loss it had been."

"Yeah, I read Mr. Ballamy's letter," I say, remembering how well-written and from-the-heart it was.

"Yes, he has been very good to our family. He has actually called both John and me a few times, and has shared some personal stories. Knowing that Emily's principal cares so much means a lot to both of us. Lisa told me after reading the letter she immediately went to Vanessa. When she went to break the news about Emily being in a special class at Twin Oaks and what had happened to her, Vanessa burst out crying and said she knew."

"So, just to clarify, Vanessa knew of Emily's condition before the letter?" I ask.

"Yes."

After a long silence, she says, "Lisa said that Vanessa hadn't known about the original accident, but found out about Em's condition shortly after Emily started attending school at Twin Oaks. Lisa confided that her daughter had been acting so strange the last few months that she was about to make an appointment with a counselor to find out what was wrong. Vanessa was eating poorly, didn't want to go to gymnastics, and stopped wanting to hang out with friends."

I can understand that feeling of shutting down, of not wanting to do anything because of sorrow. I can't imagine, though, how an eighth-grader could possibly process something so terrible as a friend who was totally fine the last time you saw her and now was wheelchair-bound and unable to speak.

"Lisa said Vanessa had learned of Emily's condition from one of her classmates, who apparently goes to your class as a peer tutor," Ms. Thompkins says. "It seems like different kids would share stories about Emily or other students from your class. With each story, Vanessa felt more and more guilty. That's when her mom said she began to change."

She pauses again, so I share, "We do have a lot of peer tutors that come into our class. It's been of mutual benefit—the Special Ed and Gen Ed kids really appreciate their time together. Did Vanessa eventually come to our class though? I don't remember a peer tutor named Vanessa joining us."

"No, Lisa said her daughter never came. My gut reaction when I heard that was one of anger. Who was she to tell me that her daughter wasn't doing well, when it was my Emily who had lost so much? She couldn't muster up the courage to visit her old best friend? She should have been there for my little girl the first time."

I hear a little sniffle. Ms. Thompkins' tone softens, "Mr. Smith, as soon as those thoughts entered my mind, though, I broke down crying on the phone with Lisa. I felt so bad being angry at Vanessa. She was always so sweet and full of life . . . a really good friend to Emily. I knew it wasn't her fault for falling out of touch as the years passed. And it certainly wasn't her fault for never having heard about the accident the first time if no one told her." Her voice cracks as she completes her thought: "And as for not visiting these last few months, how can I blame an eighth-grader for feeling scared and not knowing what to do? I mean, John and I are adults, and we still didn't fully know how to feel or act at times with our Emily. How can I expect a middle-school girl to make more sense of this crazy, unfair life than I'm able to?"

I nod my head, though this conveys nothing over the phone. "I guess after Vanessa found out about Emily, there was a lot of hidden, self-inflicted guilt and no healthy outlet for processing any of it. Lisa told me that she found out later that it was during Vanessa's lowest week that her Language Arts teacher invited her whole class to attend that time of remembrance that you had set up for Emily. Vanessa's plan was to stay home sick or take the study-hall option the teacher offered as an alternative. For whatever reason, though, Vanessa got out of bed that day, went to school, and decided that she needed to go to the observance."

I go through a mental file of people at the memorial, and a face comes to mind. "Ms. Thompkins, have you seen Vanessa recently? Could you describe what she looks like?"

"I haven't seen her recently, but she is quite distinctive-looking. Vanessa is very tall and skinny, like her mother. Lisa shared that she has taken to wearing all black, almost like she was in a constant state of mourning."

I was right. Vanessa was the girl who shared the story about playing games like M.A.S.H. with Emily toward the end of the ceremony. I wondered how she could speak about Emily in such an intimate way. It all makes sense now.

"Yes, she was there," I say.

"Lisa said Vanessa came home crying, but looked like a girl who had a weight of guilt finally lifted from her shoulders.

She told her mom about the words that were shared, and how everyone recognized that the life Emily had lived, even after her accident, was meaningful. It was 'just perfect' she said. Vanessa told her mom about the moment of silence you requested and how the classroom that had been full of loud, unfamiliar sounds became suddenly still. 'You could hear a pin drop,' she had shared. I didn't know anything about the ceremony, other than you were probably going to share the two pictures of Emily that I dropped off in the school office. I knew my girl was special, but I had no idea that so many other people besides me recognized it.

"When you told me about the time of remembrance, I didn't think I wasn't ready to hear more words about my Em, especially from those who only knew her after the accident. But hearing about everything from Lisa, even hearing the stories third-hand, has helped bring some peace. I guess something special does happen within those classroom walls."

As I tell Ms. Thompkins how much I appreciate her call, I hear Mr. Ballamy's booming laugh behind me. He makes his way around the classroom, giving fist-bumps and small Tootsie Rolls to each student who wants one. Ms. Thompkins recognizes the laugh and speaks with new warmth, "It sounds like you have a visitor. Is Mr. Ballamy checking up on the kids?" I compliment her on her laugh-recognition skills.

While watching Mr. Ballamy interact with my class, I marvel at his growth in comfort with our students since the beginning of last year until now. I comment to Ms. Thompkins, "I'm kind of jealous of Mr. Ballamy. This year he has become like the cool, fun grandpa who drops in with treats and then leaves before having to deal with the consequences of sugared-up kids."

Ms. Thompkins laughs briefly, perhaps realizing it has been a while since anything close to lightheartedness was hers. Suddenly, her voice lowers and resumes a more serious tone. "Well, besides filling you in on what Lisa told me, there is something else that I need to tell you."

"Oh, okay . . ." I say, fearing what words I might hear next.

"I already told Mr. Ballamy, but I wanted to let you know as well, that our family is dropping the lawsuit against the school district. I don't know how much that was worrying you, but I thought I should be the one to let you know."

I am stunned. Speechless.

"Even though it wouldn't be unreasonable to file a lawsuit, I know I can't hold onto this anymore," she says. "I need healing, not constant reminders in court of everything that went wrong."

I can hear the lump returning to Ms. Thompkins' throat. "I know myself, Mr. Smith, and I know I'm not one to let go of things nor one to extend forgiveness, but I need to this time. I know that is how Em would have wanted it after her last few months spent with you all. Whenever I think about pursuing litigation, I can almost hear Emily saying, 'Geez, mom—you just gotta let it go!' She used to say that to me all the time when I'd get angry about something or someone when we were together." She starts to cry. Speaking through her tears, she remembers, "Even when I was most frustrated, Emily always found a way to calm me down. I loved how good-natured and big-hearted my daughter was."

Ms. Thompkins insists this time that she needs to let me get back to my class, but wishes to share one last thing about

Emily. "She really was an angel, both before the accident and afterwards. Did you know her middle name was Grace?"

I have my eyes closed, biting my lip, trying to hold my emotions together.

"Yes, Emily Grace Thompkins. She showed grace in her life, and in her memory I am going to show grace, too. What choice do I have? That's the only thing she would have wanted as her lasting legacy."

I am overwhelmed. With her extension of grace, Rachael Thompkins changes everything. As we end our conversation I'm feeling a mixture of gratitude, sadness, relief, and respect, but not knowing how to put that into words I simply say, "Thank you, Ms. Thompkins. Goodbye."

"Goodbye, Mr. Smith." Click.

I look down, wipe a tear from my eye with the front of my thumb, and then swipe the sweat off my forehead with the back of that same hand. Jan is looking at me with a concerned expression. "Everything okay there, Mr. Smith?"

I clear my throat and give a close-lipped smile. "Yeah, everything's all right, Mrs. Jan." I look around the room and see Molly sitting in her chair gently rocking. A peaceful expression rests on her face. I then turn my attention to the whole class. "Sounds like morning meeting is wrapped up— good job, everyone." I grab my stack of outdoor, entertainment and sports magazines, as well as the pictures of travel destinations I had printed before the phone call, and head to the front of the class. "We will be working on summer collages this morning," I tell my students.

As Mr. Ballamy crosses my path to head to his next appointment, he gives me two solid pats on the shoulder. "Keep it up there, Mr. Smith," he says softly, but with confidence. Then he says louder and with mock seriousness, "And if I hear about Stephanie being extra-goofy like last time I was here, I want you to report her to me. Understand?"

Stephanie bursts out laughing and brings both hands to her mouth. "Ooohhh!" is the sound she produces as she acknowledges the joke and her lack of fear for a leader others find downright intimidating.

"Thank you, Mr. Ballamy, I'll make sure to let you know," I say in reply to this banter that is new to our working relationship. Mr. Ballamy can't help himself as he makes a V with two fingers and points to his eyes, then Stephanie's, twice, a la Robert DeNiro in *Meet the Parents*. Another "Ooohhh!" and a burst of laughter comes from Stephanie. Mr. Ballamy smiles, then as if remembering Emily once again, his face droops, and he gives a big sigh.

CHAPTER TWENTY

IT HAS BEEN A couple of weeks since I have talked with Pastor Tim, who counseled me through the initial days after the accident. I get him up to speed with what's been happening—the time of remembrance for Emily in the classroom, Ms. Thompkins' unexpected call, and the remarkable grace she extended to the district, the school, and to me.

"Tim, I know we don't normally talk much about spiritual matters during our sessions, and I have always appreciated how you've never pushed that with me, you being a pastor and all."

Tim responds that he figured that the conversation would evolve naturally when I was ready. Looking at the floor, I let him know I am ready today. Tim settles back into his chair, still in an attentive pose, but also signaling non-verbally that he would not be jumping in. It was now time to tell my story.

"I was in church almost every Sunday since I was a month old, and I was good at playing church. If there was a memory verse in Sunday School, I could recite it perfectly. If the teacher asked a question, I usually had the right answer. As we learned about the 'rules' God wanted us to live by, I remember at a young age being confused by some stories, like when Jesus told the people when doing acts of charity not to let your righteousness be seen by others. He said something like, 'When giving to the needy, don't let your left hand know what the right hand is doing.' "

I look up at Tim as if asking if he was familiar with the passage. He just nods to show that he is following me, and I realize I probably don't need to do Bible-story check-ins with a pastor.

"Of course, Jesus didn't mean this literally, but as a kid I was genuinely perplexed by this command. I remember one time during Kindergarten Sunday School, I held onto my offering so tightly in my right hand that there was no room for the money to breathe, let alone be seen by my left hand. I put the coins in the offering basket as it went by and wondered, *Did I pass the test?*"

While I'm talking, my mind flashes back to Dr. Givens' question, *Do you have excessive concerns about being morally right or wrong?*

I continue on with my story. "In a way, Tim, I think I never stopped trying to do everything right. Never stopped trying to clutch my offering tight enough so that I wasn't messing up. I think one day, during my junior year of college, I realized that church and God had become one big cycle of trying to always do right, always feeling like I failed, and then trying to get back into His good graces. Eventually it all became just too draining."

I'm not usually a person who processes things out loud, but as I talk through my past with Pastor Tim, it was the first time I could see the dots connecting between my obsessive thoughts and my beliefs—my compulsion to dwell on every mistake, my over analysis of every action in every situation, and how that ultimately caused me to drift away from my faith.

I wait for Tim's response and can tell he is formulating his thoughts as he looks out the window. Finally he breaks the silence. "I'm sorry, Michael, I wish I could have known you twelve or so years ago as a middle-school student and we could have talked about forgiveness, and dug deeper into what that looks like for *you*. Not for the right Sunday School answers, but for *you*."

I listen and can feel my chest rise and fall with each breath.

"Let me ask you this," Tim continues. "When one of your students does something wrong, how do you respond?"

"I guess I always try to teach the students to apologize, try to make it right, and then we all move on together." I picture Stevie's head on Stephanie's shoulder after the doll-out-the-window incident.

"The follow-up question for you, though, is how do you *feel* about your kids after you see them doing the wrong thing?"

This time I recall seeing Devonte put a classroom *Garfield* book in his backpack. When I asked him about it, he cupped his hands over the side of his eyes, at first too ashamed to admit what he had done. We talked about taking things that aren't ours, and Devonte retrieved the book and was truly apologetic. Even while talking about stealing, I wanted him to understand that I was proud of him for his attitude.

A third image of our peer tutor, Cory, came to mind. She had come back from such a dark place, and I couldn't wait to see her in our room again working with Justin—back to where she belonged all along. I tell Tim that, honestly, I rarely ever feel anger or disappointment while at work. Usually the only emotions I feel towards the kids are happiness and pride.

"Michael, listen," Tim says, "you're a nice guy, but you make mistakes, get self-centered, and have your shortcomings like the rest of us. You've shared stories about your class throughout our time together, and all I ever hear is love, joy, and a protective care for your kids. Now if that's you, and that is how you feel about mistakes done in the classroom, how do you think a God of love feels about you?"

I sit in silence, looking at Tim, who returns my look with a gaze that communicates how much he believes what he just said. "I think sometimes we hear sermons and read books trying so hard to understand who this God is, or, like you said back when you were going to church, if you are living up to the standard He has for you. But the truth about God that I go back to is, 'The LORD is merciful and compassionate, slow to get angry, and filled with unfailing love.' Maybe going back and seeing through a cleaner lens what God thinks about you will help you on your journey of trying to figure out what you think about Him."

These words resonate as true to me. I look directly into the pastor's eyes and say, "Thanks, Tim, I will think about all of this, I promise. I probably don't say it enough, but thank you for everything. I mean it."

Tim smiles back. "You got it, Michael. Now, if you ever want to hear more of my ramblings, feel free to join us on a Sunday morning. The doors are always open to a good Boston sports fan like you."

I laugh as I stand up and extend my hand toward his.

CHAPTER TWENTY-ONE

EVERY NOW AND THEN I like to put my music library on shuffle and see what comes up. There's nothing like a song that can transport you back to a certain time, place, or memory.

This morning, after a nice middle school flashback of Sister Hazel's *All for You*, the more random *Little Drummer Boy* came up next. I was about to change it, because listening to a Christmas song in June felt odd, but it was the version performed by Bing Crosby and David Bowie, so I let it play on. I kind of forgot how much I loved this version, with Bowie only four or five years removed from his makeup-laden Ziggy Stardust days, and Bing Crosby, a classy, clean-cut singer who hit his fame in the 1930s and '40s. I remember hearing once that no one knew it at the time, but Crosby was only five weeks from the end of his life when he recorded his last special. Here was the ultimate odd couple—two singers who couldn't be any more opposite in personalities, music styles, and stages of their careers, yet they came together and formed something amazing. What they created resonated with people so strongly that, forty years later, it is still in constant play during the Christmas season—or in June when your playlist is on shuffle.

*   *   *   *

The students are working hard on their Language Arts Velcro file folders. It's always great to see the students working on these types of assignments, because the tasks are right at their levels, and there is a feeling of independence each of them experiences while completing their folders. For Stevie, it is working on matching upper and lower-case letters. Devonte, who is at a slightly higher academic level, has work in his folder focusing on phonemic awareness. His current assignment has pictures of common items, which he has to match to the correct beginning letter sound. This one requires a little more help, but Devonte is still able to complete the majority of the folder correctly without any assistance. For our students who require help or prompting for so many different tasks, I believe it is freeing for them to be able to finish a task from start to finish on their own with little or no adult intervention. You can see the pride in their faces, and their self-esteem rising, as they complete a folder and raise their hand knowing they are going to be praised for a job well done.

During this time my role is more or less to float around the room, giving the occasional reminder, or helping a student who is stuck get back on track. While doing my walk around the room, Cory comes up and asks if she can speak with me. I tell her, "Sure," and we step aside from the main working area and meet near my teacher desk in the corner of the room. "What's up, Cory? Is everything okay?"

"Well, not exactly," she says averting eye contact and looking toward the floor.

I don't know what it is about that one motion of her casting her eyes downward, but the negative messages start to steamroll into my brain once again. I can feel my temperature rising and moisture starting to form near the top of my forehead.

I take a breath and try not to repeat any mantras or look ahead to when I can escape to the bathroom. As I had done previously with Luke's sister, Stacey, I am now trying to ride out the wave of anxiety preparing to sweep through my body. It is time to acknowledge that I can't read Cory's mind and that, either way—sweat pouring down, or not—it is more important to hear what she has to say than to have total composure.

The sweat starts to bead up, and I can feel the tightening around my major muscle groups. Cory begins to talk, and I try my best to focus and listen. "It's about Justin," she says. "You remember a few weeks back when he screamed and hit Stevie in the face?"

My face is flushed, but I am curious about what she is saying, and I can feel my mind start to shift from calculating my anxiety levels to concentrating on Cory's observations. "Yes," I respond. "Is everything all right? Are you feeling nervous about Justin after his incident with Stevie?"

Cory takes a quick glance up at my moist forehead, but her eyes don't linger there. "No! Not at all!" There is fire in her response, as if she is upset with the notion that anything or anyone would prevent her from working with Justin again.

I smile, wipe the sweat off my forehead, and refocus my mind's attention back to Cory. "What were you thinking about then, Cory?" I ask with genuine interest.

"Well, it's more of what I noticed that day, and what I am noticing today as well."

I encourage her to explain further.

"You know how Justin always goes like this—" Cory imitates looking up and staring at the ceiling lights with her fingers placed slightly above her right eye, rolling her fingers up and down like four separate waves. Suddenly, she looks embarrassed. "Oh my God! I wasn't making fun of him. You know I would never do that, right?"

I give her a reassuring smile and say, "No, Cory, I didn't think for a second that you would ever make fun of Justin. It is just a self-stimulating behavior that helps calm him."

"Okay, good. Yeah, I would hate myself if I ever made fun of any of my friends. But anyways, I know Justin always is doing that finger-thing, right? But on that day he hit Stevie, he did something different. Remember, I was sitting with him right there?" She points over to Justin's desk near the side of the room. "We were just hanging out while you were doing that money store thing."

I tell her I remembered everything she described very well.

"Well, on that day," she continued, "he was doing his finger-thing, then all of sudden he stopped moving his fingers, and took them and hit his head like this." Cory demonstrates the independent waves of separated fingers suddenly stopping, then, after closing the three center fingers together like a tight fence, she unexpectedly gives two quick whacks to the right side of her head. "He did just like that," she says, "then he started doing his finger-wave-thing again. I don't know for sure, since, you know, Justin doesn't really talk, but I think he was telling me his head hurt last time. I noticed it for the first time like five minutes before he did what he did to Stevie, and it's not like it happens all the time, Mr. Smith.

In all the time I've worked with him, I only saw him do it that day—that is, until he did it just a minute ago."

As one, we swivel our heads and look at Justin. He is looking squarely at Cory but no longer doing any stimming. He is forming his hand just as Cory described, and quickly strikes his right temple. I don't doubt Cory's instincts. I have never seen that motion before, and wouldn't have noticed it now if she hadn't pointed it out.

"I know I'm just a kid," Cory says, "but I think Justin's telling us his head really hurts."

I am stunned. What incredible insight from an eighth-grade student who had been kicked out of our school only one year prior! As I look at Justin, I am amazed that his eyes, which are fixed on Cory, are communicating so much. If this behavior is a precursor to something major that is about to happen, I know the time to act is now.

"Jan and Barb, I think it might be a good idea to take the kiddos outside to recess ten minutes early." The adults and students do not know the reason for this, but better to be safe than sorry. As the kids are lining up, I see Justin complete the pattern two more times, smacking hard at the side of his right temple with three closed fingers. He stares off into space, and then, just as Cory predicted, his body jerks with that familiar terrible movement, as if electricity had just torn through his brain once again—then comes the ear-piercing scream! Stevie, at the classroom door, covers his ears with both hands and looks at Jan with a fearful expression. Jan gives his back a comforting rub and helps usher him and the rest of the kids quickly out of the room.

With foam mat in hand I move toward Justin, ready to protect his face. For the first time in two years, because of the surprising friendship between this Crosby-Bowie duo, we had an idea of what was going on with our hurting student.

*   *   *   *

Cory's observation ends up being a game-changer. Now that the antecedent and function of the behavior is known, the corresponding behavior intervention plan is easier to develop. The school district's behaviorist comes the following day and talks with Jan, Barb and me about how to be proactive, as well as sharing some ideas on how to better calm Justin once he crosses his threshold of pain.

Pam, our assistive technology specialist, adds a new icon to his communication device that allows him to inform us when his head hurts. We positively reinforce him for using his "voice" and are figuring out options to relieve his pain before it becomes unmanageable. Justin now has more motivation to use his voice output device. We start taking him to the quiet therapy room, where we discover that the spinning swing, as well as massaging his head with some pressure squeezes, helps to calm him. Nurse Nancy receives written permission from Justin's mom for us to administer a half-tablet of Advil when he communicates that his head hurts, and that seems to make a big difference.

We are working together as a team, and I feel good about better meeting Justin's needs. I am also indebted to one fourteen-year-old girl who didn't know anything about antecedents, data collecting or Functional Behavior Analysis reports to get us "experts" on the right path.

CHAPTER TWENTY-TWO

IT IS EARLY AUGUST, almost a month and a half since eighth-grade graduation. Though I am enjoying the break and time to recharge, I miss the kids, too.

It is a happy surprise when Justin's mom emails me and says this has been his best summer yet. Once he understood how using the communication device helped him get his wants and needs met, he began to express himself more. It has been especially valuable for signaling when his head is beginning to hurt, but also to make specific food requests and what he wants to watch on the computer as well. She closes her email with, "I had no idea that my son loved watching old Looney Tunes clips on the computer so much . . . It's awesome!!!"

I hear that Pam, who is very excited about Justin's increase in communication, will meet with him and his mom the week before school starts to program more social communication phrases into his device. This will help him increase his social interactions as he moves on to Edgefield High. While thrilled to hear about what a successful summer he has been having, I'm also a little sad that this might be my last "Justin update," as we rarely get to see or hear about our kids after they leave our program.

An even more unexpected contact is when I run into Ms. Thompkins at Trader Joe's. I approach her as she is looking at some pasta sauces. It's always a little disorienting when you see someone out of their usual context, but she also seems somewhat panicky when I greet her.

We start off the conversation with casual talk about our summers. We agree we're both looking forward to the opening ceremonies of the Olympics that Friday. I tell her a little bit about the end of our school year, and how her friend's daughter, Vanessa, started coming into our classroom as a peer tutor two to three times a week.

"Yes, I actually did hear about Vanessa's time in your class through the grapevine," Ms. Thompkins says. I tilt my head, puzzled. She clarifies by adding, "I heard the news from Lisa. We've . . . reconnected, and it's been a good thing. She even told me that Vanessa invited one of your students to come over to the house to hang out. It was all Vanessa's idea."

I am stunned. "Wow—really? That's great! Who was it?"

"I believe she said her name was Stephanie. The girl's mother also came, because Stephanie had never been invited to a friend's house before. Lisa said the mom looked more nervous than her daughter, but within five minutes the two girls were laughing and looking at teen fashion magazines in Vanessa's room."

Ms. Thompkins smiles wanly as she tells the story, and I wonder what memories of Emily may be bombarding her own mind as she talks about the developing friendship between these two young middle school girls.

"You know, Ms. Thompkins, I've been wanting to tell you how much your kindness and forgiveness meant to me." Her eyes shift from looking off into the distance back to me. She gives a faint smile to acknowledge what I am saying. I decide to press forward with my question that I hope doesn't sound trite nor invasive: "How are you doing?"

She closes her eyes and gives a heavy-hearted sigh. "It's not easy, and some days are worse than others, but I'm in a good support group." She then looks up and to the left, as if considering whether to say more. "Mr. Smith, I'm glad we happened to meet today. It sounds strange, but I really needed this."

Surprised, I respond, "Oh? Why is that?"

"It's just that I have been afraid to run into you ever since the school year ended—not just you, but anyone from Twin Oaks who would remind me of those last few months with Emily. When I go into town to do any shopping, the first thing I do is scan the store quickly to make sure no one is there that I don't want to see. I've been talking to my support group about it lately, and they think my anxiety is fueled by the fear of not knowing how I would react to someone who was a physical reminder of losing Em.

"Actually, I feel embarrassed for being so worried about this, but when I first saw that it was you who called out my name, my forehead started to perspire like you wouldn't believe! You must have thought I was a wreck. After we got into talking about summer plans and Lisa, I think I started to calm down."

Ms. Thompkins has no idea how much I can relate to her feelings of distress. Looking at her forehead, I can see a little sheen, but nothing obvious. I reassure her, "To be honest, I really hadn't notice anything."

"Good. My support group will be happy to hear that things weren't a complete train wreck, like I was convinced they would be," she says with some relief.

"I'm glad I ran into you today, too, Ms. Thompkins," I say with sincerity.

"Please, after all we have been through, call me Rachael."

I agree, and, just as we had started out several month prior, we shake hands. Her firm grip is familiar, but this time it has more complexity—it is strong, yet caring.

CHAPTER TWENTY-THREE

AS I WAIT BY the big oak tree, I look over at the open double doors I have walked through many times now for one of my sessions. I observe Pastor Tim from a distance and notice how he greets each person with a warm handshake or a small hug. Suddenly, I feel a tap on my shoulder. I turn around to see Josie's lovely face. "Hey Josie! Thanks for coming with me today," I say as I give her a peck on the cheek. We then back up for our special greeting.

—CLAP—CLAP—

We head toward Pastor Tim. Our *Top Gun* homage had gotten his attention, and he says loudly from across the narrow street, "Talk to me, Goose!" Josie doesn't get Tim's reference—she still hasn't seen the movie.

We walk up to the church's entrance and say our hellos. "Pastor Tim, I'd like you to meet my girlfriend, Josie. Josie, this is one of the most awesome people in the world—Tim."

Pastor Tim gives his familiar wide welcoming grin and shakes Josie's hand with both of his own. "So nice to meet you Josie. I hear from Michael that you are quite the teacher."

Josie looks down and smiles, blushing slightly. "Well I'm still learning, but that's very nice of you to say." Her humility despite her obvious teaching gifts has always been so attractive to me.

Pastor Tim then turns his attention back to me, "It's really good to have you here, Michael."

"Yeah I think it's been a long time coming," I confess. I look over at Pastor Tim and then over at Josie, and think to myself how thankful I am for the support of these two people standing next to me.

We small talk a bit longer outside, and then get ready to head into the building. "All right, Tim, we'll see you inside. Good luck! I mean, not that you need luck preaching a sermon. Ummm, I mean, God bless you?" I'm a bit rusty with church-speak, and a little more nervous about attending a Sunday service than I had originally thought.

Tim laughs and says, "I appreciate your well-wishes. Hey, pay close attention to the first part of the sermon. There is a nice 2004 Red Sox reference in there that I think you will appreciate."

We all shake hands again and then make our way to the balcony stairs. *He's got to be talking about Curt Schilling's gutsy performance. That sports moment would make someone believe in miracles, for sure.* I think about our miracle-moment when Molly sang to Devonte on his birthday even though she was on sensory overload. Can't believe I only have her one more year before she heads off to high school.

We scoot our way along the first pew in the balcony section and find an open seat next to an older gentleman and his small, thin-limbed wife, who reminds me of the Rapping Granny in the movie *The Wedding Singer*. After we have settled in, Josie whispers to me, "So what are these special lunch plans you talked about?"

"Well, since our first date was a few weeks back and I was too nervous to eat, I decided to make up for it."

Josie shakes her head, remembering our dinner together at the Daily Catch restaurant. "Yeah, Michael, you asked if we could split a dinner. I was thinking, 'Who works up the courage to ask a girl out, but then only wants to pay for her to eat half a meal?' "

I can't help but laugh at my own stupidity in that moment. "I wasn't trying to be cheap, honest! I couldn't believe that I actually got to be on a date with you, and got a nervous stomach. It was a compliment, I think."

Josie looks down and smiles. "Okay, I'll take it as a compliment."

"So, to make up for that first-date blunder, I thought we could go back to the North End and split one of those giant seafood-filled pans from Giacomo's."

Feigning disbelief, Josie teases, "So we are still splitting a meal? Michael, this is not looking good."

"No! I mean, yes, we are technically splitting a meal, but it's a gigantic meal! No sane person would attempt to eat it on their own!"

Josie nudges me with her arm and says, "I'm just kidding, Michael. That sounds really nice."

The music starts, and the chatter of the congregation subsides. I recognize the guitar chords as a more contemporary version of an old hymn that was my Grandpa's favorite, "It is Well with My Soul." Josie leans over for one last comment before the service starts— "I will pray that you don't get nervous and fail to eat your half of the meal."

"Amen," I say, nodding my head in agreement.

*   *   *   *

During the greeting time, I watch as Josie effortlessly interacts with the gray-haired couple to our right. I know she still volunteers once a week to visit some elderly folks who have a difficult time getting out of their homes. As she talks, I think back to the last day of school. We were both finishing packing up our rooms, and I stopped by her classroom to say goodbye. We talked a little about how unforgettable this year was for the both of us, and I thanked her for everything she did for the kids, and for me personally. She just shook her head as if to say it was nothing. When I asked if she and Bobby had any big plans for the summer, she looked down and said quietly, "Bobby, ummm . . . he actually broke up with me last weekend. He said the long-distance relationship was just too hard on him."

While I wanted to pump my fist and shout, "Yes!" that seemed a little tactless, so I just responded, "I'm sorry about that."

I think back to the previous summer after our first year of teaching and how I really missed Josie during that time. Even though we weren't as close that first year as we are now, I remember how I missed running into her in the hallways, hearing her funny stories, talking with her about different students, and especially her goofy sense of humor. Now I can call her up, and we can just talk, or plan a date in beautiful Boston whenever we want. Sometimes she sends me funny YouTube videos, like Jimmy Kimmel hooking up kids to fake lie detector tests, which she finds hilarious. She's also someone I can easily confide in when I'm feeling anxious. I still can't believe I'm the lucky guy who gets to spend my time with Josie, reading books together on the Boston Common, or looking down on the city from the top of the Prudential Building on a clear Friday night.

CHAPTER TWENTY-FOUR

SO I GUESS THIS is where my story ends, at least for now. There hasn't been a miracle cure, or a three-easy-steps-to-overcome-social-anxiety program that I passed. I used to stand in my shower four years ago, hot water pouring over my face, and wonder what book I had to read, what medication I had to take, or what realization I had to have to get back to my old self—before eye contact and anxiety became my dreaded companions.

The difference between now and then is I'm at peace with the current chapter of my story—one where I still take prescribed medication, still seek counseling periodically, and still get nervous about upcoming events. And if I run into you by chance in a Dunkin' Donuts line, you might notice me starting to sweat and wonder why I'm having trouble making eye contact with you at first. Most of the time, though, I won't try to run away from our social interaction. Internally, I will be riding that wave of anxiety until I'm able to carry on the conversation normally, or what I accept as normal for me.

I think the best part for me, though, is that I appreciate the everyday moments again—talking with people, enjoying time with Josie, and throwing my head back and laughing soundlessly. I am also thankful to be back in church again.

Emily touched the students in our class, and the other staff and students at Twin Oaks, in a profound way. Eventually, rumor has it that our school district and the

Thompkins family will be presenting an annual "Emily Thompkins Grace and Bravery Scholarship" honoring a student who is beating the odds and touching the lives of those around them. If that happens, I can easily picture Cory contending for that award.

*   *   *   *

At one of Pastor Tim's sermons later in the summer, he posed a question that stuck with me—"Imagine God showed up to you one day and he said you could talk to him or pray for anything you wanted right now. It would be a Solomon-like moment, and your prayer would be answered. What would you talk about or what would you ask for?" Tim stayed silent for a short time, giving his question time to breathe with the congregation. Frankly, I forget the larger point of his sermon, but I do remember my reaction to that question.

I recall thinking that, if God approached me, I would ask him first about Emily. How was she? Does she know the impact her fourteen years of life had on so many people? Then, for my prayer, I would ask that Justin's headaches would get better and that he would keep making progress with expressing his thoughts, and that Devonte and Stephanie would develop more friendships with other kids from the school. I would pray for Molly, that she would conquer her fears and find peace, and for Stevie, to one day hold a job where he could use his great people-skills to positively impact an entire community. I'd pray for Rachael, too, that her broken heart would continue to mend.

I then find myself reflecting on my response, realizing that it was the first time in a long while that I hadn't hoped or wished or prayed for the "old me" back. Thoughts about eye contact, sweat and anxiety levels consumed me, but I am now starting to get my eyes off myself and onto others again. For this I would have to give thanks to a caring pastor, an insightful therapist, a supportive General, a grace-filled parent, a trustworthy friend, a kind-hearted dreamgirl, and, of course, the amazing students of Classroom A113.

Acknowledgements

First, I want to thank my Savior, Jesus, who has walked alongside me and shown me so much grace and love throughout my life.

I want to recognize my wife, Jenn, who was the inspiration for the character Josie, and who is the kindest and most quietly hilarious person I know.

Much appreciation goes to my mom, Lois Smith, who worked many hours to refine and edit my manuscript. She is a retired Speech-Language Pathologist, and was the one who encouraged me to consider Special Education as a profession following my time as a high school peer tutor.

To my other family members and friends—your encouragement, times hanging out, and inside jokes make up some of the favorite parts of my life. That includes my grandma who is the true storyteller of our family . . . I will always value our "talk story" times.

Special thanks to my friend Eric Bodiroga who did an excellent job designing the book cover. I also appreciate the work of Todd Lawson who edited my final manuscript.

I cannot begin to list all the incredible General Education and Special Education staff, and parents, with whom I have been privileged to work with. So many of you were in my thoughts as I was writing this book. I'd also like to thank the counselors whose professionalism and caring hearts made a huge difference in my life.

Finally, I have to thank the remarkable students who have been in my classes over the last eight years. I hope that my students' caring and loving personalities, and their persevering natures, shine through the pages of this story. They are true rock stars, and I'm blessed to be able to work with them.

About the Author

This is Bradley Smith's debut title. He has worked in Special Education for ten years, first as an Instructional Assistant, and then as a Teacher in Self-Contained Classrooms or as an Inclusion Specialist. He has struggled with social anxiety, with some elements of OCD, for the past eight years.

Brad loves exploring Portland, Oregon with his wife, Jenn, and rooting on his favorite teams—the Portland Trail Blazers and New England Patriots.

Reading Group Questions and Topics for Discussion

1. Describe Michael's thoughts, feelings and physical manifestations when he is having an anxiety attack. Do you know anyone with anxiety issues who experiences similar responses?

2. If you belong to a church, how have they addressed mental health issues? Why do you think Michael feels comfortable talking with Pastor Tim?

3. What do you think of Pastor Tim's suggestion that Michael try to put his experiences into multiple "drawers" on page 15, instead of just two?

4. Do you think the trajectory of Michael's life would have been different if he hadn't had the encounter with the stewardess who had intense eye contact?

5. Why do you think Cory and Justin bring out the best in each other, even though they are an unlikely pair of friends? Where do you see Justin in five years? Where do you see Cory?

6. Michael says that his classroom is a "judgment-free zone." Do you agree that there are very few places, if any, where you don't feel judged while in middle school? Do you think that social pressures increase or decrease later in life?

7. Mr. Ballamy's attitude toward the kids in A113 changes over the course of the story. Have you observed people who found compatibility with others whom they once found "different" after getting to know them?

8. What qualities does Josie Liu possess that attracts Michael to her?

9. Can you see yourself in any of the students portrayed in this story? For example, Stevie is high-energy and friendly. Stephanie is faithful to her boy-band and not deterred by what seems unattainable. Molly is timid, but pushes herself beyond her comfort zone. Justin is a puzzle, but shows good potential once the right systems are in place for him. Devonte has an impressive knowledge of baseball trivia that can build bridges with others. Emily's life was changed in an instant, but she also impacted others' lives.

10. What were some of the strategies that Pastor Tim taught Michael to use when he became anxious? Why were they not the most helpful for him? Do you think they could still be useful strategies for other people?

11. Dr. Givens' suggestion that Michael has some components of OCD shifts the way he thinks about himself. Do you know anyone who has heard difficult news, but once getting past the initial shock was thankful to know what they were facing?

12. When Michael finally saw the string of urgent text messages about Emily's allergic reaction at the zoo, do you think his physical and emotional reactions were the same or different from his typical reactions when he was anxious?

13. Communication is an underlying theme in this story. How did the styles of communication evolve for Michael, Mr. Ballamy, and Rachael Thompkins? How did the ability to communicate change for students like Emily, Justin, Molly and Vanessa?

14. Has your view of Special Education or students with special needs changed after reading this book? If so, in what ways?

Made in the USA
Middletown, DE
16 March 2019